Be Human Like Jesus

Be Human LIKE JESUS

DAN · IVINS

BROADMAN PRESS
Nashville, Tennessee

© Copyright 1988 Broadman Press

All Rights Reserved

4250-49

ISBN: 0-8054-5049-1

Dewey Decimal Classification: 232.8

Subject Headings: JESUS CHRIST - HUMANITY // CHRISTIAN LIFE

Library of Congress Catalog Number: 88-324

Printed in the United States of America

LIBRARY OF CONGRESS
Library of Congress Cataloging-in-Publication Data

Ivins, Dan.
  Be human like Jesus / Dan Ivins.
    p. cm.
  ISBN 0-8054-5049-1 (pbk.) : $3.25
    1. Jesus Christ—Humanity.   2. Christian life—Baptist authors.
I. Title.
BT218.I95 1988
232'.8—dc19   88-324
                                                                   CIP

To Daisy,
who taught me much
about loyal companionship,
and was as aware of my
humanness as anyone,
yet loved me in spite of
it . . . to the end.

Acknowledgments

I want to express gratitude to Mrs. Angie Grooms, who has spent most of her life giving of herself to people in service to God, who spearheaded our visit to Israel, and thus provided the impetus for writing this book. Also, to the congregation at the Baptist Church of the Covenant, by whom I passed most of the ideas and whose rich diversity, openness, and willingness to dialogue enhanced the final composition. And especially to Mrs. Sarah N. Wilson, whose love and commitment to excellence is an inspiration to me.

Dan Ivins
Birmingham, Alabama
August, 1987

Contents

Introduction

I was forty-three years old before I ever made a pilgrimage to Israel. All my life I had envisioned what it must be like to be in the place where Jesus grew up, taught, ministered, died, and was raised from the dead. I went with the National Conference of Christians and Jews. It was an experience I shall never forget.

One of the places we saw was Caesarea-Philippi in Galilee. That was not only the site of the headwaters for the Jordan River but the place in the New Testament where Peter made his famous confession of Jesus as the Christ.

> He said to them, "But who do you say that I am?" Simon Peter replied, "You are the Christ, the Son of the living God." And Jesus answered him, "Blessed are you, Simon Bar-Jona! For flesh and blood has not revealed this to you, but my Father who is in heaven" (Matt. 16:15-17).

"You are the Christ!" said Peter. I know of no stronger statement of the divinity of Christ than this, unless we consider Jesus' own testimony: "I and the Father are one" (John 10:30). At the outset, I want to affirm the deity of Christ without question because it is a nonnegotiable part of my own theology.

But the humanity of Christ is equally nonnegotiable. That is the purpose of this book, to speak to the humanity of God in Christ. Once we recognize Jesus' humanity, I believe it can encourage us and provide us an example to live by. For the truth is, God wants

9

us all to be human like Jesus. He wasn't so caught up in being God that He couldn't also be human.

Jesus was a down-to-earth God. Don't take that lightly, for it is a radical truth. It means that at one time in history God lived here as a human being. The eternal One entered time; the invisible One became visible; He whom we once thought of as "in heaven" was once here on earth in Jesus.

If God had wanted to avoid being involved with humanity, He would have avoided the incarnation. John's Gospel begins with these words: "In the beginning was the Word, and the Word was with God, and the Word was God" (v. 1). But John reached the climax just a few verses later, "The Word became flesh and dwelt among us, full of grace and truth" (John 1:14).

God's coming down to earth means involvement, relationship, and intimacy. We can know Him, and He can know us. God is no longer just absolute but particular, no longer just abstract but concrete.

Jesus Christ is the concrete expression of an abstract God. He "is the visible expression of the invisible God" (Col. 1:15, Phillips). He came so that we might know what God is like.

But He also came down to earth so He could know what we are like. He came to live as one of us. He became what we are, so we could become like Him. He limited Himself to identify with us. Jesus Christ knew what it was like to live in a family, to be mistreated, betrayed, and misunderstood. He knew what it was like to work with His hands and to be thirsty and tired. There is no problem common to any of us that Jesus did not experience, including death.

One of the most moving religious stories I ever read was written by a German minister shortly after World War II. The Nazis had wrecked the world, destroying property and lives. There were people with no homes, no income, and no hope. The postwar years in Germany were desperate days, and it was against that background that the story was written. It was an effort to determine who was responsible for that terrible conflict.

So a trial was held and many fingers of guilt were pointed: to Hitler, the Jews, and the common person who in apathy allowed it to occur.

Finally, someone accused God, and all agreed. Surely, God was the one because He began this miserable world in the first place. Then the court promptly found God guilty and passed the severest possible sentence—God must live on earth as a human being.

Three archangels were charged with carrying out the sentence. The first said, "I will see to it that God is born on the back side of nowhere, in a country ruled by a foreign power. He will be born in a barn to a peasant girl, out of wedlock, and, worst of all, I'll see to it that He is Jewish." The second angel said, "I will see to it that God lives in insecurity all of His days and knows firsthand what torture is. He will have no place to lay His head, His family will forsake Him, and people will misunderstand Him." The third angel said, "I will see to it that God knows the horror of death. He will be killed like a common criminal between two thieves."

And then the story slows down with nothing but an eerie silence, for suddenly the people realize God had already served this sentence! He knows what it's like to be human, with emotions like us. This book is an effort to identify the humanness of God, so we might know Him better.[1]

But I want to be sure and recognize the caution my friend Janet Teitsort gave me: "Don't make God too human. Make Him grand enough to save me and human enough to feel my pain." I think that is the proper balance. The Christian God is a down-to-earth God who came to redeem real people.

1

Born of a Woman

(Gal. 4:4-5)

If you and I were to start a new world religion like Christianity, we might want to establish our leader as a mystical kind of god/man. We would provide him with supernatural powers and origins. Most likely a human birth would not be suitable. If we were to take our cue from science-fiction writings, an otherworldly origin might call for a visit from heavenly beings who would leave something behind: something that is unearthly like a cocoon, a pod, or some nonhuman source for our messiah's birth.

The last thing we would expect to be left behind would be one of us: a human being. Yet that is exactly what the New Testament says happened. "When the time had fully come, God sent forth his Son, born of woman" (Gal. 4:4). "Born of woman"—that's how Paul put it.

However, the New Testament reflects diversity in understanding Jesus' beginnings. Mark, our earliest Gospel, begins with the baptism of Christ and does not mention Jesus' birth. John goes all the way back to the beginning: "In the beginning was the Word, and the Word was with God, and the Word was God. He was in the beginning with God" (1:1). Then, "the Word became flesh and dwelt among us, full of grace and truth" (1:14). This is the loftiest view of the beginnings of Jesus.

Matthew and Luke employ birth narratives. Matthew emphasized Jesus' human ancestry in the first 17 verses of the Gospel. Our Lord, Matthew said, was a flesh-and-blood human being.

God brought Him forth from diverse ancestors like Judah, Rahab, and Manasseh. But this didn't affect Jesus, nor did it make any difference in the way He lived. He was not compelled to reproduce any part of them. He was free to be the kind of Son that God intended Him to be. Jesus was a product of His own decisions, and we have the same freedom over our own lives.

Both Matthew and Luke told the story of Jesus' birth with signs of heavenly approval and angelic choruses. Matthew wrote about Herod and the Wise Men, and Luke wrote about the shepherds in the fields. But both reported the story of Jesus in such a way as to emphasize the *human* way that God entered our world. Jesus was carried by Mary of Nazareth and born in a specific historical setting in Bethlehem in the midst of poverty. He was the child of modest parents. "You shall call his name Jesus, for he will save his people from their sins" (Matt. 1:21). This was Matthew's way of saying that heaven had intersected with earth, and earth was to be redeemed.

Paul concurred. "God sent forth his Son, born of woman, born under the law, to redeem those who were under the law" (Gal. 4:4). Born of a woman, like every other human being. Born under the law, like other Jews of that day. Jesus was subject to the domination of the very system from which He came to deliver us.

Paul was like Luke in tying Jesus' birth with a woman. Women were vitally involved before Jesus was born. Luke's first two chapters sound like appropriate conversation in an obstetrician's waiting room. Messengers shocked both Elizabeth and Mary with birth announcements. Gabriel shocked Mary more than Elizabeth with her birth announcement. Elizabeth was just old; Mary was a virgin!

Then the two got together. The old woman, pregnant with John, and the young woman, pregnant with Jesus. The child in Elizabeth's womb kicked when the sound of Mary's voice was heard. Finally, Elizabeth delivered her child, and Mary had hers in Bethlehem. OB-GYN talk if I ever heard it!

But the New Testament writers turned gynecology into theology, and obstetrics into biblical revelation. The Creator created in Elizabeth, barren and advanced in years. Zechariah, her husband who was old too, was struck dumb. He said, "For I am an old man" (Luke 1:18). Zechariah asked a perfectly natural question: "How shall I know this?" (Luke 1:18).

Then Mary was greeted with "Hail, O favored one, the Lord is with you!" (Luke 1:28). Mary was apprehensive of this smooth-talking messenger with his flowery salutations. She wondered about it and pondered in her heart "what sort of greeting this might be" (Luke 1:29). And that's natural, for who knows where divine surprises might lead? Any mother-to-be will be anxious about her pregnancy, with some mixture of joy and fear about the future. This apprehension of Mary's was well founded, and it lasted a lifetime.

Thus, Christ came when the time was full and ripe. He came not when He was wanted but when He was needed, not when the human heart was ready but when it was weary, not when religion had triumphed but when it was failing.

Christ's Birth Was Decisive

Jesus was born, in the fullness of time: born of a woman. What difference did it make? How decisive was the birth of our Lord? When He was born in Bethlehem, many decisive elements were at work. Caesar was on the throne. Rome had a vast empire with legions trampling over every road. Any realistic mind would have pointed to such powerful forces as the determining factors of the world. But in the face of such raw power, Paul said: "When the time had fully come, God sent forth his Son, born of woman" (Gal. 4:4). What influence could a tiny baby have in the face of the might of Rome? Born of a lowly mother in obscure Bethlehem on the far fringes of the empire. It would have been madness then to have believed that two thousand years later millions of people would be gathering to worship in the name of Mary's Baby!

This is the staggering part of Jesus' birth—that something so tiny, so unpromising, so vulnerable, and insignificant can be so decisive. A lot of decisive infants have been born. Think of that slave girl in Egypt, who held in her arms a tiny infant for whom there seemed no hope at all. She constructed a floating cradle and shoved him out among the crocodiles and the reeds of the Nile to survive or perish. But in retrospect, what immense issues in the world went floating down that river among the bulrushes! Moses was one of the influential babies of the world.

In our own country during the last century, the forces of disunion were threatening our nation. In frontier Kentucky, a woodsman and his bride built a rough cabin on Nolan's Creek, and there a baby was born. Who can imagine what America would be like today without Abraham Lincoln? Another influential infant was he.

Who thought anything important had happened when a black Baptist pastor in Atlanta named King fathered an infant boy who was to open the door to the most amazing civil-rights accomplishments in modern history? A baby again proved to be decisive.

There have been many influential babies born in our world. But none more than the infant born to Mary and Joseph of Nazareth. How can being like Jesus help us be better humans? I can think of several ways.

Our Need for Hope

First, it speaks to our need for hope when things aren't going our way. When human babies have it in them to be decisive, you never can tell what might happen. We might make a difference ourselves. With a baby, you never know. Around the corner in some crib may be an infant who would push open the door of a new era.

Babies are weak and helpless and have to be constantly cared for. But babies grow up in a world like our own. When the limits have been reached, when forces seem irreconcilable, when we least expect it—some liberator is being born to be a savior. The Roman

Empire crumbled and fell to the ground, but two thousand years after Christ was born, multitudes still sing, as though it were a contemporary event: "O holy Child of Bethlehem!/Descend to us, we pray;/Cast out our sin, and enter in,/Be born in us today!"[1] If you and I are to believe in the creative forces to which the future belongs, we must believe in something newborn, something inconspicuous, something now growing among us. Who doesn't need to hear that today?

The Wise Men symbolized this truth. They believed in something small when everything great was all around them. They could have bet their lives on the zodiac, but they ended up at the crib of a baby. Herod believed in brute force and raw power. What a little man Herod was! The Wise Men believed in a baby. They embodied the best wisdom that you and I can have at any age. They did not put their trust in Herod, nor Caesar, nor Caesar's legions. They did not believe in the imperial power that loomed so large and seemed so permanent. They did not rely on the obvious, the wealthy, the gigantic, and the overpowering. They believed in what God was doing in a newborn baby. That is the mark of wise persons: those who followed the star until it stood over a place where something "born of woman" lay.

People Matter

When "God sent forth his Son, born of woman" (Gal. 4:4), God was putting His trust in humanity. The birth of Christ says to all of us: *people matter*. Each time the world seems to reach an impasse, lo and behold, a child is born, and a new way opens up unsuspecting hopes.

I have a concern here. I don't doubt so much that you will deny the truth of what I'm saying, but I do fear that you may deny that it applies to you. Someone may be thinking: "This doesn't have anything to do with me at all. I am not a decisive baby. I am no messiah for whom the world stands waiting. I am just an ordinary person."

If this is where you are, consider what it takes to make any infant decisive. No baby can grow up to be great alone. What decisive persons like Christ have done is to draw things together and focus those things that other people have identified. A decisive life bursts into a burning flame what had already been there but was at loose ends and uncoordinated. Jesus couldn't have accomplished what He did by Himself. God and multitudes of people helped make His life decisive.

Jesus was the catalyst where "The hopes and fears of all the years/Are met in thee tonight." That could be something of what Paul meant when he employed the phrase "Fulness of time" (Gal. 4:4, KJV). Before that time became *full,* a lot of plain people had to come first. Prophets like Isaiah caught a glimpse of it six-hundred years before Jesus ever came (Isa. 9:6). He saw a foreshadowing of the gospel greater than the world had ever known, where "The wolf shall dwell with the lamb" (Isa. 11:6). John the Baptist came to prepare the way, to "make straight in the desert a highway for our God" (Isa. 40:3; Luke 3:4-6). But all these preparations were in the air at the time when Jesus was born of a woman. The time was full. Think of all the other people who helped make Christ decisive.

Think of Joseph, who took a risk on Mary and her Baby. And Mary herself: What if she had just said no instead of: "Let it be to me according to your word" (Luke 1:38)? What about the scholars in the Temple who took the boy Jesus seriously? What about His friends in Bethany who supported Him during His down times? And what of the twelve disciples, who gave up all they had to follow Jesus? Multitudes of people—with God working through them—made Christ able to be great. We cannot have decisive babies without other people around, folks like you and me. When Christ was "born of woman," God was saying that. Thousands of people had to "Prepare the way" before the decisive Messiah could walk up with salvation in His hands and say, "Here it is!" All of us matter. Personality counts. That's what any of our being "born of woman" means. What personality in your life needs to be made great?

Many decisive babies have been born, but none greater than Jesus of Nazareth. How decisive is He to you? Every person alive ought to answer that. What difference has Jesus' being "born of woman" made in your life?

When I came as pastor at The Baptist Church of the Covenant for the "trial period," I laid out the platform which would serve as the base for what I could be expected to do if I became their pastor. I took my text from Paul's letter to the Corinthians, "What we preach is not ourselves, but Jesus Christ as Lord" (2 Cor. 4:5). It was my way of saying that Jesus Christ is decisive for me. Everything I do as pastor, hopefully, is based off that text because it embodies how decisive Christ has been for me. In determining my moral approach to life, how I go about doing church, my life-style, my understanding of patriotism and community, Jesus Christ is decisive.

There was a time when this was not so. I have been directed by the past and tradition. I have been other-directed, living by what other people might think. But for some time now, I have been struggling to be a faith-directed Christian. That is because I made Christ decisive in my life.

So whether something or someone is decisive for us depends on our relationship to it and its relationship to us. How decisive is Christ in your life? The poet got close to what I mean when he wrote: "Though Christ a thousand times in Bethlehem be born, if he's not born in thee, thy soul is still forlorn."

The angels in heaven recognized how significant Christ's coming was, but others around were oblivious to it. The shepherds saw His being "born of woman" important enough to leave their flocks, but to those people in the inn who crowded Him out, He didn't mean anything. How decisive is Christ to us? How differently do we live because He was "born of woman"?

The coming of Christ was decisive. We agree with that. Any-

body who could bend the datelines of history around an unpreten-
tious stall was decisive. He has it in Him to be decisive. Is He
decisive to you? Christ is decisive only to those who make Him
decisive. Some do. Some don't. Some did. Some didn't.

While Rome was busy making history, caught up in all the
activities of history making, God came, and Rome missed it. God
came and pitched His fleshly tent on straw, in a stable, under a
star. The world didn't even notice. It didn't miss a lick. It kept right
on running; the engines of commerce kept moving along. The
world was reeling from the wake of all the greats: Alexander the
Great, Herod the Great, and Augustus the Great. Thus, the world
overlooked Mary's little Lamb. It still does. I hope you won't.

2

Tension at the Temple

(Luke 2:41-52)

Growing up in a family guarantees tension. This was evident early in Jesus' life too. Not only was He forced to flee the wrath of King Herod by going down to Egypt as a baby, but in His childhood He met conflict on His trip to the Temple at twelve.

This time it was not with Herod, His enemy, but with Mary, His mother. However, the cause of the tension had to do with His Father. We meet it in two Scripture passages of Luke's Gospel: "Son, why have you treated us so? Behold, *your father and I* have been looking for you anxiously." And, "Did you not know that I must be in *my Father's* house?" (2:48-49, author's italics) Two fathers are the topic of conversation between a mother and her Son—one human, one divine. It appears that only Jesus recognized the distinction that day, which surely led to some of the confusion in that scene.

Nevertheless, Jesus was caught in the middle of a conflict between His mother's love and His Father's business—a form of family tension that is familiar to all of us. We pick it up at the Temple in Jerusalem when Jesus was only twelve years old and just beginning to move out of the dependency stage and into the tension it creates in family life. Joseph had brought his family to the Passover, and they had finished the celebration and were on the way back home to Nazareth. But Jesus stayed behind, engrossed in a deep spiritual hunger with the teachers of Judaism.

His parents didn't even discover that Jesus was absent until the next day.

We Can Lose Jesus

This incident indicates a danger that is inherent in being a disciple of Jesus: we can lose Him! His parents did. They lost Him when their interests were other than His interests. The result was separation. I find it significant where they lost Jesus. They lost Him in a religious congregation, where many today, I'm afraid, have also lost Christ. But also look where they found Him. Mary and Joseph found Jesus in a religious congregation, where many others have found Him as well. "After three days they found him in the temple, sitting among the teachers, listening to them and asking them questions" (Luke 2:46).

That says a great deal about the interests of the adolescent Jesus. It also says something about the wisdom of those rabbis in the Temple, and what it says is good. What a fine thing they did in taking time for this boy! Jewish leaders still do that today. One of the highlights of a trip I took to Israel was to be in on a bar mitzvah for a twelve-year-old boy named Russell Vinik at a synagogue in a kibbutz in Galilee. Rabbi Steven Glazer of Birmingham was continuing that fine tradition begun in Jesus' day. Those rabbis listened to Jesus' questions, and they answered Him. When they asked Him questions, they listened to His answers. This went on in a religious congregation, and that is always a good experience.

A Mother's Love

But all this religious interaction was rudely interrupted by two frantic parents, including a mother who was obviously frustrated, and she chided her Boy: "And when they saw him they were astonished; and his mother said to him, 'Son, why have you treated us so? Behold, your father and I have been looking for you anxiously'" (Luke 2:48). Who can blame Mary for this normal response? She let Jesus know in no uncertain terms that she cared about Him deeply by her intense anger at His irresponsibility. By doing so, she gave Jesus something to strive for, something to react against, something to struggle with, and something to grow away from. That is a valuable gift for any mother to give her child.

When Jesus said, Did you not know "that I must be about my Father's business?" (v. 49, KJV), it was a gentle but firm reminder to Mary of the first sign of conflict between mother and Son. It came from the pull of the call from His Father, which somehow Jesus was already sensing at twelve years of age. But it clashed head-on with the protective instincts of His mother, who was worried for His safety. The protective love of His mother was one side of the tension.

Mary seems to be portrayed by Luke as a mother who was loving but protective. That's not so unusual, considering all Mary had gone through to bring Jesus into this world. She paid a price of shame and misunderstanding from the way Jesus had been born, so it is only natural for her to shield Him from harm.

The Father's Business

But over against this is the pull of what Jesus spoke of as His "Father's business." This is not defined clearly by Luke. But it could be referring to that influence which called Jesus beyond the boundaries of His mother's small world of protectiveness, out into His Father's unknown areas of concern. Jesus' curiosity at the Temple represents a force in His life at a very early age that tended to pull Him away from His mother.

The Temple episode was only the beginning, for this yearning within Jesus continued to grow as He ventured out in the name of His Father's business, causing one controversy after another. And His Father's business led Jesus to square off against the authorities of both Rome and Israel. And in the end, Mary's worst fears came true as she witnessed her Son executed on a cross like a criminal.

So from Mary's perspective, she must have asked: "What has all this silly talk about His Father's business gotten Him?" And Mary wound up exactly as the angel had said, with her mother's heart pierced through by the sword of suffering (Luke 2:35).

So both of these tensions were present in Jesus' life and are true of us as well. A mother's love stands for that part of us which is concerned about security and safety. This protective instinct that most of us got from our mothers stays with us a long time. It keeps us from being too reckless at times and can be helpful in growing up.

However, what Jesus called His "Father's business" is also a part of each of us. This is the creative instinct, the call of curiosity, adventure, and growth that urges us to move out and take risks. It is the business of His Father that calls us out to get involved in activities where the end is not clear from the beginning.

I don't want to be dogmatic about these tendencies. We must recognize that mothers can be risk takers as well as fathers. And fathers can be as overprotective as mothers. But these two traditional roles of mothers and fathers are perceived as being generally true. It becomes a mother to give love and sustain her child in a protective way. It becomes a father to bring forth the potential that is in every child and to challenge and inspire them to be creative. The point is, the same two forces that had a lot to do with shaping Jesus' personality are the same kind that mold us. And how we regard them and respond to them is crucial, no matter how young or old we may be.

We need to be a balanced person like Jesus. In my opinion, if we listen only to the protective side and are controlled by a mother's love, we may never venture forth and mature as we should. On the other hand, if we are always launching out, risking the unknown, being about our Father's business, we may do something "extreme."

The Israelites experienced this in their journey through the wilderness. When God called them to go forth to claim the Promised Land, they sent out spies. They listened too long to their mother's love and concluded that the risks were too great. They would stay where they were, which is sad. But notice what actually happened as a result of their standing still. In their attempt to protect life, they lost it. And those who were unwilling to risk perished in the desert, where they chose to remain. Taking the Promised Land fell to their children, who were capable of taking chances with the unknown. These were the ones who possessed the Promised Land.

Now we are into one of the deepest lessons in the Bible and in all of life. Jesus mentioned it frequently: "He who finds his life will lose it, and he who loses his life for my sake will find it" (Matt. 10:39). This is exactly what happened to Jesus. Emboldened by the love of His mother, He went out in the name of His Father's business, beyond the security of His mother's love. But there He trusted the security of His Father's love and said, "Father, into thy hands I commit my spirit!" (Luke 23:46). It was in venturing forth that gave His mother's love meaning.

The Dawning of a Conviction

Here in Jesus' very first recorded words in the Bible, we meet the imperative of surrender: "Did you not know that I *must* . . .?" (v. 49, author's italics). Do you catch the note of discipline in these words? They don't sound like words of freedom and liberty that we like. Perhaps Jesus was not totally free, totally loved, or totally protected, but He had enough of each to live successfully.

Who said He *must* be about His Father's business? Who was forcing Jesus to do that? What kind of legal code of compulsion was putting the screws on Jesus? I can think of a few. One was love that whispered, "I must be about my Father's business." It was duty that affirmed, "I must be in my Father's house." It was a sense of purpose that rang out, I "must work the works of him who sent me, while it is day." It was compassion that sounded the word, I "must needs go through Samaria." It was the voice of sacrifice that claimed, "The Son of man [must] be lifted up." It was the peal of victory that shouted, On "the third day" I will "rise again"! This imperative *must* is used thirty-eight times about Jesus and His mission. We could do with a little more of that ourselves.

Mary, bless her heart, didn't say, "Now, Son, Mother knows best." Although she did not understand her Son, she kept an open mind and a good memory—two handy tools for any parent. "They did not understand the saying which he spoke to them" (Luke 2:50). How rare is the person who realizes that you can learn more if you don't try to understand too soon. Rarer yet is the parent who can open a discussion without closing it. How rarely mothers lead with a light rein with their kids, and how unusual is the child who can voice expectations for the parents as readily as the parents can voice theirs for the child.

Notice that Jesus obeyed His parents. "He went down with them and came to Nazareth, and was obedient to them" (Luke 2:51). The dawning consciousness of Jesus' unique relationship to God and seeking His life's calling did not keep Him from minding His parents. It did not make Him too proud or haughty. Jesus was no less an earthly Son because He had a divine Father. The fact that He heard heaven's imperative did not mean He should ignore earthly allegiances. And being about His Father's business did not abrogate Joseph's business in the carpenter's shop in Nazareth where Jesus worked for eighteen more years. And because of that, "Jesus increased in wisdom and in stature, and in favor with God and man" (Luke 2:52). So should we.

3

No Deals with the Devil

(Matt. 4:1-11)

No one is immune to temptation—not even Jesus. By virtue of His incarnation, Jesus was susceptible to being tempted as all humans are. But He made no deals with the devil. Rather, He wrestled with the tempter. It is recorded by the evangelists, so we can observe how one Human conquered the temptations before Him.

Some cannot believe Jesus could be tempted or that He was so perfect temptation wouldn't take Him on. I believe the temptations were genuine. Jesus was really tempted—"one who in every respect has been tempted as we are, yet without sin" (Heb. 4:15). If the temptation experience was not authentic, then Jesus wasn't really human. For the struggle with evil remains integral to every human experience. It lies at the heart of what it means to be human, namely, the agony of choice. Choosing evil may seem an easy thing, but living with the consequences is not so easy. That's what makes temptation such a precarious adventure.

Several observations can be made about the Gospel accounts of Jesus' experience with temptation. First, the story could only have come from Jesus Himself, since nobody else was there to witness the struggle. It must have been something Jesus wanted us to know, or He wouldn't have shared it.

Second, the temptations were messianic. All three offered first-century alternatives to being the Messiah. Jesus chose none of them. Instead, He took his cue from Isaiah (61:1-2) and laid it out the first time He preached in His hometown synagogue (Luke 4:16-18). Jesus was not faced with simple, clear-cut choices between good and evil. In each case Jesus was tempted to do a good thing. But each time Jesus rejected the good in order to do what was better. Evil is subtle like that.

Third, the temptation narrative is thoroughly Jewish. The early church explored particular issues in Jesus' life in terms of Old Testament events. Matthew had already made a comparison of Jesus and Moses (Matt. 2:13-15). Now Matthew portrayed Jesus as the New Israel.

Just as Israel was tested "forty years" in the wilderness in preparation for entering the Promised Land, so Jesus spent "forty days" in the Judean desert. Israel failed, but Jesus emerged victorious. By demonstrating that Christ experienced personally the trials Israel underwent, the Gospels declare that God's redemption is once more in motion. Jesus' obedience and victory redeemed Israel's disobedience and failure.

Because the temptations were pivotal to the Gospel writers, they were placed early in each account, like a portent of what was to come. For they recur again and again in Jesus' life (Matt. 16:23; Matt. 27:40). They show up in the decisions He made, the mighty deeds He accomplished, and the teachings He shared. They are a revealing interpretation of Jesus and His ministry because they show the human way Jesus went about fulfilling His calling. Therefore, they become important in guiding us for our day.

The tempter begins with an attack on Jesus' most vulnerable point: His identity. He had just come from the Jordan and heard, "This is my beloved Son, with whom I am well pleased" (Matt. 3:17). That was a high and holy hour. Now He went to the desert where He hears another voice, "*If* you are the Son of God, . . ." (Matt. 4:3, author's italic). That "if" is where the rub comes in. Humans meet it on every occasion something monumental or even ordinary is being undertaken. In Jesus' case what was being tested was not the worst but the best: His faith and commitment.

That makes it very hard to hang tough because it's difficult to hang onto anything when your calling is being questioned and all odds favor your failure.

No Deals with the Materialistic

Reminiscent of the manna event in the wilderness (Ex. 16:4), Jesus' first temptation was about food: "Command these stones to become loaves of bread" (v. 3).

In shaping an answer, Jesus recognized that choosing something good meant ignoring something better. People were hungry and needed to eat. But Jesus knew they needed something more. Religion involves far more than our stomachs.

Our church has begun a soup-kitchen ministry to help feed the street people in Birmingham. Five days a week they come through our doors to eat a free and nourishing meal. We realize that they are hungry. But we also know they do "not live by bread alone" (v. 4). So in addition to the meal, we share our faith by praying or reading a Scripture verse while they eat. It is our way to say that food is important, but God is more important.

Do you see the subtlety of the temptations? To do something good sometimes means to leave undone a greater good. So many of our solutions to problems are aimed at the symptoms but leave the diseases untouched.

Jesus responded by quoting from Deuteronomy 8:3. He taught the lesson that went unlearned by Israel: trust in God and God's sustaining care. There is a greater source of nourishment that deserves every human effort: seeking and doing God's will. Seeking that first will override lesser things (Matt. 6:33).

So it was no deal with materialism for Jesus. He saw that way of being the Messiah as temporary and unworthy. Movements founded on the material will ultimately collapse. All America saw it happening before their very eyes as the televangelists declared "holy war" on one another. It revealed a ministry built on materialism and greed. This is not what Jesus had in mind when He said,

"The gates of hell shall not prevail against it" (Matt. 16:18). A material kingdom will never last. It takes more than bread to meet the deepest needs of human beings.

So Jesus refused to provide bread, but it had less to do with a lack of compassion than a recognition of priorities. People have to live but they also need something to live for. By rejecting the tyranny of things, Jesus refused to forsake the cross for a bakery.

No Deals with the Miraculous Sign

The desire for signs of power is the issue of the next temptation (Ex. 17:1-7). Israel had sinned in the desert by demanding miracles from God as a sign of God's power. But Jesus trusted in God's care and chose to forego the need for miraculous proof of God's love. Jesus refused to make demands on God.

If no bread was to be offered, then how would Jesus find followers? Why not "throw yourself down" from the Temple? (v. 6). The temptation was to win a following as a miracle-working Messiah. People would surely respond to that kind of leader. They do it every day. The two professions most susceptible to the miraculous are religion and medicine, with politics coming in a close third. Quacks in these fields rake in billions of dollars.

Recently, there was a movie about fooling folks called *Critical Condition*. Richard Pryor played the part of a con man who is posing as an experienced doctor in an isolated medical unit in New York City during a hurricane. "Doctor" Pryor acts so well in the chaos that he fools nurses, patients, and doctors alike, finessing his way in and out of one healing situation after another. Then he is faced with performing back surgery. But before being exposed, the entire community sees him as a miracle-working healer, simply because he wears a white coat and a stethoscope around his neck. I think the film is a statement about how badly human beings yearn for the miraculous. Some people will believe anything!

But Jesus would make no such miraculous deals because He knew that people are not really changed by the spectacular. His answer to the tempter (drawn from Deuteronomy 6:16) teaches the lesson of confident trust in God's providential care. Convictions go deeper than our eyes. God cannot be found by magic tricks (Acts 19:13-16). Utilizing the supernatural would enslave people and take away their freedom of choice. In Jesus' refusal to rely on the sensational, He was reaffirming the incarnation. When God came to us, He came through the back door, not to impress us but to redeem us (Matt. 1:21). We see later how Jesus called the disciples to follow Him, not for the spectacular glory which they could see but for the service they would render. By this unusual strategy Jesus invites us to follow God, not because of showmanship but as a result of His sacrificial service.

No Deals with the Militaristic

The third temptation, that of idolatry, Jesus also countered with a quote from Deuteronomy 6:13. Unlike Israel who lost faith in God and fabricated a safer, more visible object of worship (Ex. 32:20-33), Jesus taught the lesson of faith in the unseen but powerful, true, and only God.

If Jesus would not use materialism or miracles to fulfill his messianic calling, why not use the military? That was the most popular expectation, and He would have had little trouble pulling it off. Why not start a holy war, a righteous crusade and make the world safe for Judaism—or today—Americanism? Why not invade some foreign country and show our strength and power over the other kingdoms of the world? It is a universal and modern temptation, still very much alive.

Once again the answer comes back: religious battles are never fought with the tempter's weapons. Jesus could not fight for His messianic crown with a sword or the weapons of war. He found a better way to defeat Rome than military force. The "weapons" of Jesus were faith and sacrificial love, never a sword.

Check your history books for the verdict of the choices Jesus made at the outset of His ministry. Israel did choose to take up the sword against Rome, and they lost big in the first century. I've climbed on foot up to Masada, in the desert overlooking the Dead Sea. Masada was the last bastion of resistance against the Romans, which ended in mass suicides. So it wasn't long until the entire nation of Israel and its Temple were reduced to utter ruins, staying that way for nearly two-thousand years.

But the early church did follow its Lord; it responded to Rome with a cross, not a sword. It was much slower and more painful, but in less than three-hundred years, Constantine declared Christianity the official religion of the empire! It resulted in a whole new civilization which lasts to our own day. The way of the cross always seems to be a way of weakness, but in the long run it gets better results than the sword.

In Jesus' struggle, He inspires every struggling believer. Temptation is a part of life. It is also an opportunity to become more like the Lord. Jesus didn't have to be told about human nature. He knew what was in men and women (John 2:25). He realized that we are more than mouths to feed, a pair of eyes to startle, or citizens to be liberated. We are persons who need to be redeemed. For that to happen, there can be no deals with the devil—then or now—only commitment to the ideals of the will of God. Instead of giving people what they wanted, Jesus gave them what they needed. Jesus never put Himself in the forefront. God was always at the center of all He did: "You shall worship the Lord your God/and him only shall you serve" (v. 10).

A television evangelist in Oklahoma raised over a million dollars by seducing people into believing they would get bountiful prosperity or protective providence. Always we are tempted, lured to be sensational, impressive, and powerful. That's the way we think the world works.

There is a story about a poor migrant worker in southern California who stole fruit from the orchards at night to sell the next day for profit. One night he took his son along to hold the bag while he dropped the fruit from the trees. He came to a cross path and stopped to look both ways. After climbing up a tree he began to drop the fruit. His son, who had been attending Sunday School in a church nearby, said, "You didn't look in every direction, Dad; you forgot to look up." The man climbed down from the tree and never took the fruit again.

Jesus looked up to God when He was being lured by temptation and when He did, God directed His eyes back down to the way of service. It is the way of the cross. The very heart of Jesus' temptations, and ours too, is to escape the demands of the cross. "God forbid, Lord! This shall never happen to you" (Matt. 16:22).

There are other ways to be a messiah. They may even have some things going for them. But how can we choose a lesser good when the best is set before us?

Having to choose is also what the temptations are about. And that makes it tough to be a Christian to this day. While it is hard to be a Christian, it's too dull to be anything less. It is very hard to bear the agony of choice, but it's inhuman to refuse it.

Every Christian and every church have a choice to make. We can open soup-kitchen lines and feed the hungry. We can dazzle people and the incredulous will show up. We can identify religion with the idolatry of nationalism and the patriots will wave their flags. People will come, but will they belong to Christ? We belong to Christ by faith, not sight; love, not hate; and the cross, not the sword.

In Scott Peck's book: *People of the Lie,* he concluded that if evil is to be neutralized, it must be absorbed.[1] When evil raised Christ on the cross, it enabled us to see Him from farther away. In this way, evil backfires. This is how Jesus overcame evil with good (Rom. 12:21). Peck continued:

> I do not know how this occurs. But I know that it does. I know that good people can deliberately allow themselves to be pierced by the evil of others—to be broken thereby yet somehow not broken—to even be killed in some sense and yet still survive and not succumb.

Whenever this happens there is a slight shift in the balance of power in the world.[2]

Because the voice of God can never be silenced by any power, there is only temptation to misinterpret it. People will continue to worship with a lack of commitment, read their Bibles at a shallow level, use proof texts that are to their advantage and forget the ones that are not, and give in to the good at the expense of the best. But we must never ever sidestep the cross: it can change us all, allow us the strength to win over our own temptations, and help us to make no deals with the devil.

4
A Sense of Humor

(John 15:11)

Except for the laughing hyena (which barks more than it laughs) the only other creatures noted for laughing are human beings. Why, upon hearing something funny, does a person throw back his head, open his mouth, and with chest heaving to and fro laugh as his breath flows out in explosive puffs?

Is laughter not one of the distinguishing marks of being human? Indeed, not only are we the only ones who can laugh, but we are the only ones of God's creatures who deserve to be laughed at. Only a God with a sense of humor would have created creatures who confuse themselves with their Creator.

Unfortunately, church is not a place where we like to laugh or even laugh at ourselves. Humor has not yet been fully accepted into the Christian canon. The humor of God and especially of Christ has been hidden for some distorted reason, perhaps because it is so helpful in exposing our pretenses.

I have a few hunches why. Humor is more than joke telling or making people laugh. Rather, it is a way of noticing God above us, life around us, and the joy that ought to be within us. It is a way of looking at everything through eyes that have crinkles at the corners. Humor is seen in what we do and what we are. Thus, *humorous* becomes an adjective, not a noun. It's not just something you say or a joke you tell, but a state of mind, an attitude about life. A sense of humor is a sense of proportion. It says about everything, "This too shall pass." Humor, at bottom, is humility, and perhaps that is why it's unpopular in church. In church, pride comes easier than humility.

Real humor doesn't even have to make a point. All you may feel when you meet a humorist is: here is somebody who doesn't think more highly of himself than he ought to. Thus, you are more open and genuine when you are with such people.

Why can only people laugh? Could it be because we are made in the image of a God who is also a humorist? Is that too personal, too casual for our normally serious view of God? Nevertheless, the biblical writers speak of God in personal terms. And I'm glad they do. It sometimes shocks us to think of the infinite in finite terminology. Most of us would be surprised to read what the Bible really says about God—pleasantly surprised!

In the Bible God is portrayed unapologetically in human and personal terms. God possesses intelligence and emotions. God has purposes and preferences of which our humanity is a tiny, imperfect reflection. We have a God who entered human experience and dealt with people. Take, for instance, God the tailor, who tenderly sewed "garments of skins" for Adam and Eve (Gen. 3:21). Or God the struggler, who wrestled with Jacob and put Jacob's thigh out of joint (Gen. 32:24-25). Or God the stalker, who took the trouble to track down Jonah the prophet, whose heart was several sizes too small because he was more interested in running from God than in liberating people (Jonah 4:1-2). This is the God of the Bible, portrayed in human terms: doing what humans do, experiencing what humans experience. The God of Abraham, Isaac and Jacob, the God and Father of our Lord Jesus Christ, could be aroused with strong feelings, repenting—changing His mind, getting jealous, crying, and laughing.

God Laughs

The psalmist's God was One who knew how to laugh. Four times the psalmist depicted God laughing. And nothing is more human or personal or—dare we even say—godly, than laughter.

Have you ever imagined God laughing? The thought is not irreverent if we believe God is like Jesus. Although no place in the New Testament records that Jesus laughed, I often picture Jesus and His disciples enjoying a hearty laugh together, and I believe there is laughter in heaven. "He who sits in the heavens laughs" (Ps. 2:4). Our personal God has a sense of humor.

There must be some things that God finds funny, even things that He created Himself. I imagine that when God finished making the moon and stars, and a galaxy of suns, He turned His attention from the big things to fashion little ones: beautiful things like flowers, birds, and tree leaves that present us with a kaleidescope of colors. In keeping with His sense of humor, God even made some comical things just in case our minds should become rigid and dull, humorless and gray. To remind us not to take ourselves so seriously, God created caterpillars, cats, and ducks that waddle around. When He created ducks, I bet God smiled. Seeing those bright eyes blink surely made God laugh. And He's probably laughing still at the sound that comes out of a duck's bill. Yes, God laughs, and His humor lies in the way He regards us.

But laughter expresses many moods. There is the intense laughter of sheer delight, the hollow laughter of cynicism, and the brutal laughter that cruel people hurled at Jesus on the cross. Then there is the derisive, scornful laugh of one who gets the last laugh.

When I was young, my brother Tommy and I used to play a game we made up called, "Got you last." It usually involved tagging each other, but the game depended upon getting something on the other so we could rub it in. How creative we could be at doing that! If we were bored sitting together in the car on long rides or in church when the preacher was waxing too eloquent, we'd start playing "Got you last." I'd usually start it. I'd reach out, tag him subtly, and say, "Got you last." And he'd get me back, which meant I had to get him; on it went until one of us got tired of that! But my, how we people like to "get" one another!

The Psalmist and Laughter

This seems to be the kind of laughter the psalmist was talking about when he said, "The Lord laughs at the wicked" (Ps. 37:13). God not only laughs, but according to the psalmist, He will have the last laugh! He will be the last one to do the "getting."

Look up the word *laugh* in your biblical concordance, and you get the notion that humor is not one of the spiritual gifts most to be sought after. Old Testament laughter runs close to being pretty cynical stuff: Sarah laughing at God (Gen. 18:12), God laughing at sinners (Ps. 59:8), and somebody laughing somebody else to scorn (Job 22:19). Old Testament laughter is mostly "got-you-last laughter." The righteous got the last laugh on the unrighteous.

While I agree with that in principle, in the long run I believe good is stronger than evil. Still, there's something about this that leaves me dry. Could it be that we've been looking under the wrong word for our biblical idea of humor? I believe that a much better word than *laughter* is the biblical word *joy*. There is no cynical joy. And the Bible has a great deal to say about joy—all of it good. Joy is one of the spiritual gifts to be sought after. It was Jesus' prayer that His joy should be in His people, and that their joy should be "full" (John 15:11). The noun *chara,* which means "joy," occurs fifty-eight times in the New Testament, and the verb *charein,* which means "to rejoice," occurs seventy-three times. Therefore, one could safely say the New Testament is a book of joy. There is no excuse for the dull dreariness which so often passes for our kind of Christianity that thinks it's sinful to enjoy living. We Christians are men and women who have partaken of the good news of God. And it ought not take a humorist to remind us of God's ministry of genuine laughter.

Mostly folks think of Jesus as a "man of sorrows," and He was. But Matthew also portrayed Him eating at a dinner having a good time (Matt. 9:10-15). Jesus was happy being with His friends, helping people who needed help; and He rejoiced in His work, so

He compared it to a bridal party on a honeymoon. "Be of good cheer," he said (Matt. 9:2d, KJV). "Consider the lilies of the fields, how they grow" (Matt. 6:28). "Greater love has no man than this, that a man lay down his life for his friends" (John 15:13). "The third day there was a marriage at Cana of Galilee, . . . Jesus also was invited to the marriage" (John 2:1).

One of the strongest tests of Christian character is in what you find true joy. What makes you laugh? Is it "got-you-last" laughing, or is it sheer delight? Jesus enjoyed nature, friendship, going to parties, having a social life and a good time; so should we. And we shouldn't feel guilty when we do. That kind of joy is simply another name for the best kind of humor. But we have to go to the New Testament to find it, and that's an amazing thing about the New Testament. There are lots of bad things that happen to people like disease, heartache, rejection, and crucifixion. There is enough tragedy in it to make it the saddest book in the world. Instead, it is the most joyful! I believe it has something to do with the Author, a God who knows how to laugh.

Jesus and His Disciples Were Joyful

I discovered a striking insight on the way to this chapter. We all know that Jesus rarely defended Himself. You recall how Herod "questioned him at some length; but he made no answer" (Luke 23:9)? Jesus seldom made a self-defense. He did so on only two different occasions when He took great pains to justify His conduct to His enemies. Both times He explained to them *why He and His disciples were so joyful!*

Religious people have always had problems with other religious people who enjoy themselves. To some, being religious and having a sense of humor are antithetical. That Jesus did not fit the expected mold of a "man close to God" was clear. Those who followed John the Baptizer, like those of the Pharisees, were quite somber in their religious expression.

Jesus Didn't Fast (Mark 2:18-19)

That's why in Mark's Gospel Jesus had to defend His disciples' failure to fast as John and the Pharisees did. They fasted twice each week, whether they liked it or not. Jesus said that kind of forced, insincere abstinence is nonsense. Furthermore, He and His disciples were happy and felt no need to fast. He likened it to being at a bridal party. According to Jewish law bridal parties were exempt from fasting. So Jesus' skill in pulling this situation into His defense was shrewd. It was as if He were on a continual honeymoon and the stiff laws shouldn't interrupt His freedom and joy.

Jesus Welcomed Sinners (Luke 15:1-2)

The other occasion when Jesus defended Himself was because certain religious people complained about the company He kept. "Now the tax collectors and sinners were all drawing near to hear him. And the Pharisees and the scribes murmured, saying, 'This man receives sinners and eats with them' " (Luke 15:1-2).

Jesus told them that the work He was doing—finding lost people and turning them around—is the most joyful work in the world! I can think of nothing more gratifying than rescuing people's lives. In chapter 15 of Luke's Gospel, we read phrases like, "Rejoice with me," and "There will be more joy in heaven." Jesus said He was glad as a shepherd who found a lost sheep; satisfied as a housewife who lost a precious coin and found it; or happy as a father whose wavering son came back home. This is the kind of thing that makes the angels sing, and He wouldn't swap that joy for any kind of religious exclusivism. If He had to eat with sinners to get that joy, then eat with them He would. Jesus enjoyed Himself so much in relating to people that He had to defend Himself for being so joyful before his enemies. Think of it!

Happy People Do for Others

What do you suppose was the reason for all the joy—even in the midst of such tragedy that few of us will ever know? I believe it was because *the happiest people I know are those who do the most for others.* "My meat is to do the will of him that sent me" (John 4:34, KJV). Jesus loved life. He found life by losing it (Matt. 10:39) and defined life's greatness in terms of its usefulness (Matt. 20:25-28).

What about us? When we are called upon to sacrifice or make some commitment we usually think in terms of what it costs us or what we stand to lose. But Jesus said that a person found a treasure in a field and in his joy sold all he had to buy the field (Matt. 13:44). Jesus focused upon the joy, not the sacrifice. Spiritual treasure is worth it at any price, He felt. Do we believe that? Hardly. Only the spiritual giants among us believe in the joy of service while the rest of us whimper and complain. Paul said, "I am exceeding joyful in all our tribulation" (2 Cor. 7:4, KJV). How many of us live up to that? Very few.

Most of us grew up finding joy in getting. Thus, we invariably had to relearn how to live. Only in church do we hear that life's deepest satisfactions come through giving, not getting. Our world has to be turned upside down! Jesus' greatest joy was to help needy people, and this same opportunity is available to you and me in a thousand ways every day. Yet, how many let this treasure go unclaimed!

Jesus Brought Joy to All He Met

Have you ever checked out how often Jesus attended weddings, parties, and feasts? You ought to do it sometime; it's interesting. There are over thirty references in the Gospels to words like *weddings* and *feasts* that had to do with Jesus. No wonder His enemies said He was a "glutton and a drunkard" (Matt. 11:19)! True, it was a gross overstatement, but it would not have any validity had He not been so joyful.

I am not claiming that Jesus was on a constant high. We know better than that. There were times when He got so burdened that He withdrew from people for a short time. Once He fasted forty days. Try and match that! There were times when He gave Himself to solitary prayer, but I come back to those words: "When you fast, do not look dismal, like the hypocrites, for they disfigure their faces that their fasting may be seen by men. . . . But when you fast, anoint your head and wash your face, that your fasting may not be seen by men but by your Father who is in secret" (Matt. 6:16-18). It is incredible, isn't it? Jesus must have been the most joyful person in all Palestine. If so, how could such a vibrant soul be covered to the point that some of His churches consider it almost a sin to laugh in the presence of God? You've got me there. And we can do all in our power to change that by trying to have a *grace* church and not a *guilt* church.

Jesus Was Not at the Mercy of Outward Circumstances

But the most significant aspect about the joy of Christ to me is that it was not at the mercy of outward circumstances. The hardest part of faith is to take God as He is, to serve Him for Himself, not because we want a better job, a better marriage, better health, or to keep a loved one from dying. Sometimes we have to endure Gethsemane and choose a cross before Easter comes. But we can live in anticipation of the resurrection.

So often our attitude depends upon our goal in life. For many it is to minimize painful experiences and maximize pleasurable ones. Obviously this is better than the opposite, but it is not the goal Jesus had in mind. For Him eternal life or joy was to know God, so He prayed, "This is life eternal, that they might know thee the only true God, and Jesus Christ, whom thou hast sent" (John 17:3, KJV). Knowing God means more than knowing about Him or holding certain theological beliefs. It means experiencing God. When we do that, we receive a joy that does not depend upon what we do or is done to us, or who we are. It is a joy that the world cannot take away because it cannot give it.

You and I depend a lot on each other for satisfaction. We need each other's strokes and compliments for a sense of well-being. Many physical things in this world give us joy. To own, to buy, to share, and to relate makes how others view us extremely important. That's also why we are often disappointed and sad. That is why so many in our country today are miserable. They don't own, they can't buy, and they can't share because of tight money and unemployment. They depend upon external things for their joy.

During the last few months of Jesus' life all kinds of external doors slammed shut in His face. Had He depended upon outward circumstances for His joy He would have been the most miserable man alive. Judas betrayed Him. The crowd turned fickle. Peter denied Him. Caiaphas framed Him. The disciples couldn't even stay awake while Jesus prayed. Even His Father seemed to close a door in His face on the cross. All kinds of doors slammed on Jesus. Click, Click, Click! Every door that a person could touch was closed in His face, and He is pictured in Revelation outside the door of His church, knocking, hoping to come in (Rev. 3:20).

It was then that He fell back on resources which human hands could not reach. "No one will *take* your joy from you" (John 16:22c, author's italics). Jesus' joy was tied into a resource that was untouchable by people or circumstances. How I wish we had that! We are like yo-yos—up one week and down the next. Jesus could stand anything people did to Him and still have joy. You could put Him down, but you couldn't keep Him down. One Friday they executed Him on Calvary. Then on Sunday He burst forth from the tomb with a smile on His face. He'll come back laughing every time!

Lofton Hudson wrote about the nonverbal communication of faces. Some faces that are outwardly polite mask indifference, fear, or hatred. Some open faces invite us to be who we are. Some faces scream criticism, rejection, or intimidation at us. Many people see God with this kind of face.

Hudson told a story about Thomas Jefferson and some friends who were riding horseback in the country and had to cross a river. One bystander waited until several of the group had crossed the river and then asked Jefferson for a lift. Sure enough, Jefferson took him across on the back of his horse and set him down on the other side of the river. "Tell me," said one of the men, "why did you select the President to ask this favor of?" The man was surprised that Jefferson was the president but said, "All I know is that on some of the faces is written the answer 'no.'" Jefferson's face "was a 'yes' face."[1]

That's what the New Testament is trying to tell us about joy. Jesus Christ has a yes face. The consequences of this are significant, namely, that there is laughter in the heart of God! The deepest conviction of Christian theology is the affirmation that if God is like Jesus, then God is capable of real humor. If God and we both share some of the same problems, then we have the deepest possible bond between us; we can laugh with each other.

How can Christ with His sense of humor help me to be more human? By recognizing that true humor will never destroy anything that is genuine. All it can do is puncture balloons. Only when humor is regarded as sinful and joy regarded as unbecoming for a Christian is the church in real trouble. In this day, five senses are not enough. It seems to me that we need at least two more: a sense of compassion and a sense of humor. As far as I can tell, from a close study of the life of Jesus Christ, they go together.

5

Acquainted with Grief

(John 11:35; Luke 19:41)

Life rarely turns out the way we expect it. The last few decades have certainly not been what I had hoped. So many things I anticipated and planned for did not happen. And that goes for most people I know. The job promotion we expected and deserved didn't occur. Someone we love and trust cruelly turned out to be unfaithful. Our bodies go into a tailspin quicker than we want to believe. Our children run away from our arms. What do we have to show for it all?

Perhaps you saw the movie: *The Shoes of the Fisherman*. One scene was about a priest walking through a poor section of Rome when he was interrupted by a man running out of a house. As he ran down the stairs he saw the priest and said, "There's a man dying up there. Maybe you can do more for him than I can." The priest said, "Who are you?" The man replied that he was the doctor. "They always send for me too late." The priest went up to the room of the dying man but got no response. "It's no use," said the nurse. "He's too far gone to hear you." The man died a few minutes later, and the nurse suggested that they leave. But the priest resisted. He wanted to stay and help the family. She said no, they should go. The family could cope with death. "It's only the living that defeats them."[1]

Live long enough and you are bound to be acquainted with defeat and, thus, grief. To be acquainted with grief is to find oneself a young widow, having to bring up three children alone.

To be acquainted with grief is to experience the silent, knifelike sadness that comes a hundred times a day when you start to speak to your mate who is no longer there. To be acquainted with grief is to know the deep longing for another whose loss you cannot bear to endure. To be acquainted with grief is the helpless wishing that things were different when you know they are not and never will be again.

To be acquainted with grief is to pour one's energies for years into the struggle of making a family and to stand by seeing a beleaguered teenager shun you as a threatening enemy. To be acquainted with grief is to wake up on a sunny day with anticipation of playing your favorite game, tennis, only to be reminded by your heavy limbs that you've had a stroke. You close your eyes, now moist.

To be acquainted with grief is to invest years of your life preparing and anticipating taking your place as a minister of some church among the people of God, only to discover the vision of that anticipation and the fruits of the preparation disparaged and frustrated by those very people. We all know what it's like to be acquainted with grief.

There are no references in the New Testament to Jesus' laughing, but there are a few that have Him shedding tears. There are only two places in the New Testament that record our Master's tears: John 11:35, where we read, "Jesus wept," and Luke 19:41, "When he drew near and saw the city he wept over it." Although they are two separate instances, both passages have obvious similarities. One involved the death of a friend. The other was concerned with the blindness and willfulness of His people.

Jesus Wept

Only John's Gospel contains this story of the death of Lazarus. It shows Jesus with power over life and death, but it also shows the human side of Jesus. Jesus was a feeling person. He wasn't ruled by His emotions, but He experienced them. He took them into account. He felt things deeply, and we see how involved He became in the lives of those with whom He came in contact. Jesus wept. So should we. There are several possibilities why Jesus was so emotional, the most obvious being the loss of a close friend.

Or He could have been upset because of Mary's rebuke: "Lord, if you had been here, my brother would not have died" (John 11:32). Mary's underlying assumption here was that Jesus had failed at pastoral care. When Mary saw Him she didn't even greet Jesus. She simply asked, "Where were You when I needed You? If You had come my brother would still be alive. What kind of minister are You?" Surely this hurt Jesus deeply. Here was a sensitive soul being scolded for not being sensitive enough. So He might have cried over Mary's accusation.

But either way, He cried. The verb John used implies that Jesus burst forth into tears. It means to wail or cry out loud. My hunch is they were tears of compassion, silent sorrow, human sympathy, and authentic love. Jesus was deeply moved by Lazarus's death. His emotions got out of control. And that is the main truth of the story: how Jesus really is one of us.

Everywhere in the Gospels the story is not told by one untouched by what life brings upon the rest of us. Indeed, is it not the voice of One crying from a cross that has convinced countless numbers that God is love? Even His opponents who watched Jesus cry exclaimed, "See how he loved him!" (v. 36). So Jesus was acquainted with losing loved ones, and He cried over them as we do.

When He Drew Near and Saw the City
He Wept Over It

Luke's Gospel gives us a different context for grief in the life of our Lord. "When he drew near and saw the city he wept over it" (Luke 19:41). Of all the scenes that are portrayed in the Gospel record, few are more touching. By this time, Jesus had reached the pinnacle of success in His public ministry. He had anticipated, prepared, and worked so hard to bring the kingdom of God to all people. And now He was about to enter Jerusalem for the Passover feast. Everything came to a head in that glimpse from the Mount of Olives. Great crowds of people had gathered at the sight of Jesus and affirmed Him. "Blessed is the King who comes in the name of the Lord!" (Luke 19:38). You would think that such positive support and a glance of the beloved city would have made Jesus deliriously happy. But Luke recorded exactly the opposite. As Jesus walked across the mountain and viewed the panorama of the city of David He began to cry on behalf of the people.

Unlike John's Gospel, Luke told us the reason for the tears. It is explicitly spelled out in the next verse. "Would that even today you knew the things that make for peace! But now they are hid from your eyes" (Luke 19:42).

This word *peace* is on the lips of many today because of the nuclear threat, and it ought to be. But the *shalom* of Jesus must not be limited to that, although it certainly includes that. The "peace" Jesus spoke of is an inclusive term which catches up all the positive feelings we can think of. It includes a sense of well-being, wholeness, completeness, fulfillment, and joy. It represents what every human being wants. But Jesus' people didn't have it nor did they know how to get it. So Jesus predicted their downfall and this moved Him to tears. Do we think we are any different?

What an incredible theological image we have in this setting! Only the Christ of the Bible would cry over creation. No place else in any of the other religions do you find gods crying over the sins of humanity. The pagan gods of the ancient world couldn't care less about what happened on earth. Instead, they were more prone to anger and rejection. But only in the Bible do we find this picture of a crying God who is so deeply moved by the rebelliousness of His creation that He cries over it, rather than being apathetic or condemning.

James Dittes in his book *When the People Say No* wrote about his grandfather, James S. Freeman, who was the first minister to confide in him about his greatest problem as a pastor. Freeman confessed that he had skirmishes with the people for over fifty years. His greatest problem is still the problem for most ministers to this day: "How can I be a minister," he said, "if they will not be a church?"[2] Being a minister is like being married to someone who is not married to you. It is to take as partners those who are sure to renege. Jesus overlooking Jerusalem embodied that. The greatest Minister ever was brought to tears for those who would not let Him "gather them in." Grief comes with the territory of ministering. It is built in, guaranteed to disappoint.

I think Dittes is really onto something. He has connected the situation of ministry to deep biblical roots. Jesus captured it in Luke's Gospel when He was severely disappointed from *wanting something for people who didn't want it for themselves.* Have you ever wanted something good for somebody who couldn't care less? What did you feel when that happened? You wanted it for them worse than they did. This frequently frustrated desire is woven into the fabric of ministry.

It's woven into the fabric of living. For instance, how I've wanted to see the church teach young children about the gospel so they can grow spiritually, but their parents are more interested in their learning how to play soccer. How I want to introduce all our members to the power of prayer and the vitality of communing with God, but too often they are too busy to bother to come. How I would like to see our families grow stronger, to expand our horizons, and to see adults involved in Bible study or Sunday School, but too often many just won't get out of bed for one hour. To be more concerned for another person's spiritual growth and development than that person is, is grief work, pure and simple.

But we must not forget that this has been God's experience from the beginning. That's why He is acquainted with grief. He has always been more committed to our joy than we are. From the very first couple, through the nation of Israel to the church, it has been that way. God wants for us something a lot of people couldn't care less about, namely, a vital relationship with Him. This rejection brings Him to tears. God has been and still is disappointed by us—and yet, He never gives up. This God just keeps on wanting good things for us and we keep on rejecting them. The staying power of our God is astounding!

Yet He persists. The image of Jesus looking over Jerusalem, neither raging nor resigned but crying, is part of that unique tradition that goes all the way back to Eden where Adam and Eve took what God didn't want them to have. When God came looking for them in the cool of the day He said, "Adam, where are you?" Silence is all God got. He cries, hurts, feels pain, yet He continues. It is almost more than I can handle.

Grief Is Inevitable

So all this says two things to me about grief: God's and ours. First, *grief is inevitable:*

> He was despised and rejected by men;
> a man of sorrows, and acquainted with grief
> . . . . ;
> All we like sheep have gone astray;
> we have turned every one to his own way;
> and the Lord has laid on him
> the iniquity of us all (Isa. 53:3,6).

In these verses, one knows grief and causes grief. One day a fox chased a rabbit up and down the meadow but never could catch him. In exhaustion, the fox crawled back into the hole and complained of his hunger to an older and wiser fox, "Why can't I catch that rabbit?" "Well," said the old fox, "you are running for your supper; that rabbit is running for his life."[3]

Grief, as I have experienced and encountered it in the lives of the people I serve, can be described as people who are more like the rabbit than the fox, people who are running for their lives, not just their supper.

There are only two kinds of people: those who know grief intimately and those who are going to know it. If you haven't already, you are going to experience it. To be alive is to be acquainted with grief. Life will say *no* to us, and we had better let it when it does. We deny our many griefs at our own peril. By clinging to our previously held expectations, we deny our grief. By ignoring the fact that life fails us, that people fail us, we deny our grief. It is not to take it seriously. It is to swallow our grief, as Dittes put it.[4] And it is to fail to learn from it. Christian realism that does not deny grief or personal catastrophe is a major source of strength.

Jesus "set his face to go to Jerusalem" (Luke 9:51)—no whining, no excuse making, no complaining. Our faith asks us to face our griefs, to admit our mistakes, and recognize our problems. There are no shortcuts around Jerusalem; Jesus looked upon it and wept. We too must go through it. Why are we so afraid to cry when God isn't?

Grief Must Be Worked Through

Second, *grief must be worked through.*

> Yet it was the will of the Lord to bruise him;
>   he has put him to grief;
> . . . .
> the will of the Lord shall prosper in his hand;
>   he shall see the fruit of the travail of his
>   soul and be satisfied;
> by his knowledge shall the righteous one, my
>   servant,
>   make many to be accounted righteous. (Isai. 53:10-11).

This is painful, but it is also the amazing claim of the Hebrew/Christian faith, that God works through the grief: His and ours. It absolutely contradicts our American upbringing, our ideas of success and the easy life, and what is macho. We have a Christ who looks out over our cities, teeming with blindness, and weeps openly on our behalf because we don't know the things that make for wholeness. In the midst of our brokenness and our rejection of His good gifts, He brings salvation.

Even though He was bruised (v. 10), "my servant, [will] make many to be accounted righteous" (v. 11). That is the biblical story. He called forth His people out of slavery in Egypt and offered them deliverance. They were transients in the wilderness, taken into Exile captivity, continually breaking their covenant. In Christ, God even brought life out of the death we gave Him, which led to the establishment of the Christian church. That is God working through the grief.

The Old Testament is an account of a crying God, who experiences grief from His people time and time again. But God works through that grief to unleash the salvation that lies within it. God knows from within what it means to "see the fruit of the travail/of his soul and be satisfied" (v. 11).

Likewise in the New Testament, we have the continuation of that same type of frustrated ministry founded on broken dreams. Jesus was born in a cave, a home of animals, because there was no room in the inn. Can anything be worse than rejecting a tiny infant? And yet, that fact alone confounded the wisest scholars. Jesus came from a town that most people despised, if Nathanael gives us any indication. In His public ministry Jesus frustrated the people's expectations of a military/political Messiah, consciously rejecting that model as having any validity. He disappointed His own disciples more times than we can count.

Thus, the crowds cheering "Hosanna" on Palm Sunday abandoned Him, even as in His ministry He abandoned their expectations. He even observed the Passover meal in the presence of a traitor and finally was crucified on a Roman cross—totally abandoned, it seemed, even by God.

Do you see this twofold type of abandonment? Back and forth, God and people abandon one another. Out of it comes much grief;

and out of that, if it is worked through: salvation! Jesus both caused grief and suffered grief Himself. We, too, are causers and sufferers of grief. That is our lot. But the grief is necessary for salvation. Grief absolutely surrounded Christ's life, and I am surprised that there weren't more references to it than we have. Grief is inevitable, and it has to be worked through.

Momentum is a word that has been taken over by the world of sports. It is defined in the dictionary as "the force which a moving body has because of its weight and motion."[5] But used in the world of athletics, it refers to a mysterious sense that one team is gaining the upper hand over another team that had the upper hand. The team with the momentum takes control of the game and usually goes on to win.

Life has a certain built-in momentum to it. It shows up often in grief experiences when we encounter problems, disappointments, and losses in the struggle to find solutions. The effort to do the next thing that has to be done creates a kind of momentum and helps us to get through the grief and beyond it, only to face it again another day. We are both causes and sufferers of grief, but we have a God who works through grief—His and ours.

Church Can Help Us with Our Grief

I can think of no better "momentum manufacturer" than the Christian church. The fellowship of Christian people has the potential for getting us transients acquainted with grief and back on the track of the living. In the Christian community we have a sustaining fellowship which helps us to cope with our grief.

An interesting letter was found back in the 1930s in an old can wired to a hand pump that offered the only hope of drinking water on a long, seldom-used trail across Death Valley. "This pump is all right as of June 1932. I put a new washer in it and it ought to last five years. But the washer dries out, and the pump has got to be primed. Under the white rock I buried a bottle of water, out of the sun and cork up. There's enough water in it to prime the pump, but not if you drink some first. Pour it in and pump like crazy. You'll git water. P.S. Don't go drinking the water first. Signed: Desert Pete."[6]

"Desert Pete" indicates how *not* to handle grief. Too often our grief is self-inflicted. We gulp down the only solution to our problem and neglect to "prime the pump." We neglect preventive maintenance—coming to church to pray, worship and build up our faith. Then when we come to the moment of grief and cry out for a cool drink of water, we find that the pump has not been primed. The church is one of our best oases in this life. We can prime our spiritual pumps in church.

In one of Jesus' resurrection appearances there is this interesting development:

> Eight days later, his disciples were again in the house, and Thomas was with them. The doors were shut, but Jesus came and stood among them, and said, "Peace be with you." Then he said to Thomas, "Put your finger here, and see my hands; and put out your hand, and place it in my side; do not be faithless, but believing" (John 20:26-27).

Jesus showed them the marks of His grief and expressed His consolation. Then He left them the fellowship of the Christian faith which has been handed down to us, so we, too, may express our grief as did Thomas, "My Lord and my God!"

6

When You Disagree

(Judg. 16:28-31; Luke 23:34)

"Birds of a feather flock together." That's the way the old saying goes. And it may be true of geese and many people but not necessarily true of those who value openness and growth, because people who value such characteristics are not shattered by disagreement. I can't think of anything more human than dealing with disagreement. How many friends do you have with whom you disagree? How many "birds" of a different feather do you gather? People tend to flock to those who look, think, act, believe, and smell as they do, as well as dislike things that they dislike. It's all very natural, I suppose, for rarely do you find people who disagree and yet are still friends. As a rule, agreeing with someone is prerequisite to being a friend. That is a bad rule because people are finding it harder and harder to flock together. Ours is a mobile society, a high-tech culture, and our society is extremely diverse. There's hardly any way to avoid some kind of contact each day with those with whom you disagree.

I grew up experiencing rejection from those with whom I disagreed. Life was a contest where one either wins or loses. Sometimes one would do anything to keep from losing. Maybe that's the society that gave birth to this anonymous saying:

> To live above with those we love
> O that would be glory!
> To live below with those we know—

Now that's a different story!

Places in the Heart, starring Sally Field, is a movie about living "below with those we know," and it ends up living "above with those we love," because the hard reality is that the Ku Klux Klan does punish black people who get out of their place, and tornadoes do strike people randomly. Poverty and prejudice does go along with living "below with those we know." Such things do cause "birds of a feather to flock together."

If we are going to get along and learn to live together in our families, in our churches, in our country, and in our world at large, how do we disagree without destroying or without rejecting? How do you build without bulldozing? If you build a building, you need a bulldozer. You've got to move some dirt. You can tear down a church with a bulldozer. But you will never build one with a bulldozer. To build a church you need unity of purpose, acceptance of diversity, and tolerance of disagreement. Let us focus our attention on two young men in the Bible who were confronted with this problem of disagreement, the problem of living "below with those we know." One is in the Old Testament, one in the New Testament: Samson of Zorah and Jesus of Nazareth.

These young men, as I compared their lives, were similar in very many ways. Both of them were strong and attractive personalities. They had unusual confidence and charisma. Both made a real impact on their contemporaries. Yet because of their unusual power and personal strength, they found themselves involved from their very earliest days in one disagreement after another. Their entire lives revolved around those people who disagreed with them.

Samson of Zorah

Samson's disagreement was with the Philistines, a neighboring tribe on Israel's western border. Bad blood had existed between the Philistines and the Hebrews for years. Samson didn't help matters with all of the practical jokes he played on the Philistines. But before long the humor of the joking disappeared. Samson was burning Philistine fields with foxes' tails and killing Philistine soldiers utilizing the first "jawbone offensive" in history! Finally, Samson met his match in Delilah who enabled the Philistines to shave his hair, jab out his eyes, and make him the brunt of all kinds of ridicule. Samson was then chained to a grindstone wheel like an animal and made to walk around day after day to the taunts and jeers of the Philistines. So in the Book of Judges we see disagreement degenerating into destruction, alienation, divisiveness, hurt, and pain.

Jesus of Nazareth

In the New Testament Jesus also constantly dealt with disagreement: from the Temple at the age of twelve, where He disagreed sharply with His parents, to the age of thirty-three on the cross, where He disagreed sharply with the religious leaders. Jesus' disagreements were not as physical as Samson's until the end, but they were every bit as intense. That's because Jesus' disagreements had to do with change in religious ideas, and that never comes easy. There are folks who can tolerate change in any other area but church. You can change anything in our society—in athletics, in our schools, in our government, and in our industry—but leave the church alone.

By the time of Christ, Judaism was mostly a matter of rules and tradition. Life was relegated to minute religious details and cultic practices. Over six-hundred specific laws of what could or could not be done on the sabbath day were in effect. The essence of religion centered around washing your hands or how scrupulous you were at keeping ceremonial details.

Jesus met disagreement primarily because He tried to change all that. His approach to church was completely different. For Jesus, relationships mattered more than anything else—more than ritual, more than doctrine, more than beliefs. Relationships to God, to our neighbor, to our world, to ourselves, and to our families: these were more important to Jesus than anything else. Therefore, Jesus gave more attention to helping and caring for people's feelings than to ceremonial laws. And He spent a lot of time teaching and healing rather than fooling around with a lot of rigid religious rules. This is precisely what set Him on a collision course with the pharisaical leaders. They maneuvered His capture; they taunted and eventually tortured Him, as Samson had been treated centuries ago.

Up to this point, the experiences of Samson and Jesus of disagreement with their respective enemies were remarkably similar. But from here on, the two stand at opposite poles. The difference lay in each man's response to the way he was treated when folks disagreed with him. I want to make a comparison of something that the two men did at the point of their death. Before they died, both of them prayed, and the two prayers by these two men could not have been more disparate. You can tell a lot about a person by the way he dies. Consider Samson first.

How Samson Died

Samson was taken to a huge coliseum on a Philistine holiday so the crowds could make fun of him. Samson got the idea about doing some more bulldozing right then and there. Because he was blind, he had to be led around. So he asked the young boy who was leading him to take him over to one of the pillars and let him lean up against that structure, which was the foundation of the coliseum. While holding on to that pillar, Samson prayed one last prayer, and it was an awesome prayer. It was a specific prayer; it was a prayer for something he wanted. Samson simply asked God to remember him, for, obviously, Samson felt forgotten. Then he prayed for strength only once more to avenge his enemies. " 'O Lord God, remember me, I pray thee, and strengthen me, I pray thee, only this once, O God, that I may be avenged upon the Philistines for one of my two eyes.' And Samson grasped the two middle pillars upon which the house rested, and he leaned his weight upon them, his right hand on one and his left hand on the other. And Samson said, 'Let me die with the Philistines.' Then he bowed with all his might; and the house fell upon the lords and upon all the people that were in it. So the dead whom he slew at his death were more than those whom he had slain during his life" (Judg. 16:28-30).

Both Samson's pride and his body had been damaged by the Philistines, and his last desire was to hurt them and get even for what they had done to him. Here Samson's disagreements had become so embittered in his spirit, his grudge had gotten so strong, and he was so mad that he bulldozed the foundations of the coliseum, bringing the entire place crashing down in destruction, killing everyone, including himself. In one dying act, the bulldozer killed more Philistines than he had killed in all of his life, and in the process he killed himself, too. That crumpled heap of destruction bears stark witness to what happens when we don't know how to respectfully disagree. Building by bulldozing not only burns up those with whom one disagrees; it burns out the heart of the disagreer, too.

Centuries later, Jesus said, "Those who live by the 'bulldozer' shall die by the 'bulldozer'" (author's paraphrase of Matt. 26:52). How true that was in Samson's case. He was one who tried to build relationships by bulldozing over people. He was one who always had to have his way, and anybody who disagreed with him was wrong. That's the kind of man Samson was, until it set up a back-and-forth kind of escalation that ended in sheer destruction, both of his relationships and his life as well. The same thing happens to people today.

How Jesus Died

But what a contrast between the way Samson died and the way Jesus of Nazareth died. Jesus too had a dying prayer. He also was in the midst of taunts and mockery, but listen to the way Jesus of

Nazareth died: "Father, forgive them, for they know not what they do." Here is One who tried to build His relationships without bulldozing. Instead of His disagreements with the authorities making Jesus vengeful, they made Him more forgiving and more accepting. Jesus returned good for evil, love for hate, and hope for failure. In the face of hostile disagreement, Jesus prayed to redeem those He disagreed with. Now that is building without bulldozing.

I have concluded that most of us are better at bulldozing than we are at building. And our bulldozing has hurt children, wrecked marriages, split churches, and caused wars. In our international relationships, we choose Samson over Jesus. We write in our military manuals how to assassinate our enemies rather than to seek to negotiate with them. In our family relationships, we reject one another over trifles. In our churches and denomination, we are more Old Testament than New, following Samson rather than Christ.

From the beginning of the church, it has struggled with one disagreement after another. Even at the Last Supper, the disciples squabbled among themselves over who was going to be the greatest. Scarcely had Jesus been crucified when disagreement began to rend the fabric of the faith. Paul established a church in Corinth, and it was full of disagreement, so Paul wrote: "For it has been reported to me . . . that there is quarreling among you." Somebody says, "I belong to Paul," and somebody says, "I belong to Cephas," and somebody says, "I belong to Christ." And Paul asked: "Is Christ divided?" (1 Cor. 1:11-13). The answer to Paul's question is yes. Yes, Christ is divided because some of His people do not know how to disagree with one another.

The subsequent history of the Christian church is about disagreement, and folks are still handling it Samson's way rather than Jesus' way. Christians are doing unchristian things to one another.

Liston Pope said at Yale University once, in paraphrasing the word of Jesus, "Where two or three are gathered in my name, there shall be disagreement among them." He further suggested that

"Christianity discovered fission long before the science of atomic physics was born." We've been at it for ages. We're good at it. We are modern-day Samsons trying to build by bulldozing. Every day we are thrown into close contact with those in our families, communities, and churches with whom we disagree. It may be the color of their skin, their political ideas, or their religious life-style. Diversity exists with folks holding to valid stances concerning all these issues. If we choose to disagree as Samson did, then I see very little hope for our families, very little hope for our nation or our churches.

How then should we express our disagreements? May I recommend Jesus' way? This can lead to reconciliation and unending growth in becoming better human beings. Once again, Christ proves to be our Savior—the One who shows us how to disagree and still be friends. If we can't do that, we don't have any business trying to claim the name of Christ. We can claim the name of Baptist and bulldoze, and we can claim the name of Samson and bulldoze, but not the name of Christ. I hope that in the future we can become Jesus' disciples, rather than Samson's, and try the best we can, under God, to build all our relationships without bulldozing.

There is a story called *The Little Prince.* It tells about a fox's condition for becoming friends with the little prince. The fox gazed at the little prince for a long time. "Please—tame me!" he said. "I want to, very much," responded the little prince, "but I have not much time. I have friends to discover, and a great many things to understand." "One only understands the things that one tames," said the fox. "What must I do to tame you?" asked the prince. "You must be very patient," said the fox. "First you will sit down at a little distance from me—like that—in the grass. I shall look at you out of the corner of my eye, and you will say nothing. Words are the source of misunderstandings. But you will sit a little closer to me every day."[1]

I hope that in the days ahead we will take our cue from the fox and the little prince, and more specifically the Prince of peace. Taming takes patience and gradually earning one's trust. To barge in and control people is never Jesus' way. His way may not get immediate results, but the chances are they will be more lasting. I hope you will make a personal commitment to build your relationships without bulldozing over anybody. Try to learn how to disagree with people and still be friends.

7
When You Get Angry

(John 2:13-16)

Ours is becoming a "By-golly-we'll-sue" society. People are getting angry over things small and large. More and more people are going through life with their thermostat stuck on "hot."

A man in New York, fed up with thugs on the subway, pulled a gun and shot four youth and was hailed for his vigilante action by many other fed-ups. MADD is a clever acronym of mothers mad about drunk drivers. Families are hotbeds of anger with spouse abuse and child abuse on the increase. Growing numbers are angry about abortion, some so irate as to bomb clinics with terrorist tactics. People who do not smoke have had enough of the foul indoor air caused by smokers whose nasty habit has become dangerous.

Anger is one of the biggest personal problems we have. It is the engine that generates both the heat of rage and the ice of rejection. Anger is behind petty irritability and the cold shoulder, but it also motivates revenge and violence.

Out of control, anger has driven us to embarrassing outbursts. Suppressed, it has wounded us to the depths of depression. We regard anger fearfully because it has burned us often. Thus, we've rewritten Jesus' Golden Rule, "*Sue* unto others as they *sue* unto you!"

A seminary professor shared a case study involving a couple in which the man totally intimidated his wife. His actions soon became apparent as he continually browbeat his wife, and she

62

would sit there and take it calmly. This became a concern of the counselor who recommended a session with only the wife. When he asked why the wife allowed the husband to bully her and not stand up for herself, the counselor discovered that she did have her own ways of coping with her anger. Every day after her husband went to work, she would dip his toothbrush into the commode!

I wonder how many domineering husbands are brushing their teeth with toilet water? Mishandled anger causes things like that. It also is the result of more disrupted relationships, broken homes, aborted friendships, and wrecked lives than anything else I can think of. When people get angry they do all sorts of things, from lashing out in self-defense to sticking toothbrushes into commodes. You can tell a lot about folks by observing how they handle anger. Have you ever thought about what makes you angry?

When Jesus Became Angry

Jesus got angry more than once. This isn't unusual because anger is a familiar part of being human. Anger is rooted in our humanness, not our sinfulness.[1] The problem comes when we view anger only as a sin. We do that especially in church where we hoard our emotions. Church is filled with talk about love and kindness, and members feel bad about having, as all humans do, contrary emotions. Around church we expect things to be contained, orderly, predictable, detached, and cool. Thomas Edison believed genius was 1 percent inspiration and 99 percent perspiration. The same thing applies for the genius of faith. It was the apostle Paul dealing with a church in Ephesus who wrote, "Be angry but do not sin" (Eph. 4:26). This implies there is a kind of anger that is not sinful.

Of course, anger frequently does result in sin, which makes this common human emotion very complex. Standing alone, anger is no different from atomic energy. It is amoral—neither good nor bad. Sometimes it can be very destructive and do great harm to persons. At other times, however, anger can be creative and become an opportunity for growth and development.

Our challenge is the same as Jesus' who obviously got angry, but sinned not. He felt free to be angry, to express it clearly, and feel no apparent misgivings or remorse. It takes a real feat to be able to pull that off. So once again Jesus is our Savior in this area of dealing with our anger. On several occasions in the New Testament, I sense the wrath of our Lord, even though the word *anger* is not always used. The feelings are there, lurking beneath the surface. These are situations that involved religious abuse or social injustice.

Jesus Was Angry at the Pharisees

For instance, *Jesus practically stayed angry at the Pharisees.* Jesus felt anger at them at a place of worship, the synagogue. They got into it over whether it was appropriate to heal on the sabbath. Mark described Jesus graphically. "And he looked around at them with anger, grieved at their hardness of heart, and said to the man, 'Stretch out your hand.' He stretched it out, and his hand was restored" (3:5). That was clear, focused, creative, controlled, dynamic anger. Almost in defiance, Jesus prophetically enacted the truth He wanted to convey before their very eyes, namely, that the sabbath was made for men and women, not the other way around. People are more important than institutions.

Jesus' greatest source of anger was directed toward the religious leaders of His day. Irreligion was no problem to our Lord. It was the religious who put him to death. His scathing "Woe unto you" passages in Matthew 23 didn't help matters. "Blind guides" and "hypocrites" He called them, along with "serpents" and a "brood of vipers." Strong language! It indicates an even stronger emotional surge of anger in our Lord because of the deception of the legalistic life-style and its hindrance to genuineness in being human. Pharisees often ticked Jesus off.

Jesus Felt Anger at His Parents

Jesus became angry at those closest to Him, His parents. Living in a family gives rise to all kinds of opportunities for anger as people invariably intrude into one another's boundaries. This situation was no different for Jesus. As Jesus attempted to break away and individuate, you can feel His mother Mary tighten the reins a bit. And when she did, Jesus got angry at her being too dependent upon Him. At the Temple in Jerusalem, when Jesus was age twelve, I sense some anger underlying the comment, "Did you not know that I must be in my Father's house?" (Luke 2:49). However, Jesus still remained obedient to His parents.

At the wedding in Cana of Galilee, He got into it with His mother about His "hour." "O woman, what have you to do with me? My hour has not yet come" (John 2:4). Anger can be a demand that personal worth be recognized. When I feel that another person is about to engulf me, take me for granted, or use me, I also feel anger.

One time when Jesus' family thought He was crazy, they came to see about Him (Mark 3:20-21,31-35). Jesus response shows possible anger, "Who are my mother and brothers?" . . . "Whoever does the will of God is my brother, and sister, and mother" (Mark 3:35). In other words, Jesus was offended that His family had no more confidence in Him than that, so He adopted another kind of family, a religious family.

Jesus Felt Anger at His Disciples

Jesus became angry at His closest followers, especially Peter. At Caesarea-Philippi when Peter tried to tell Jesus how to be the Messiah, or how *not* to be the Messiah, Jesus thundered back, "Get behind me, Satan! You are a hindrance to me" (Matt. 16:23). Again, it was a matter that had to do with religion, the common first-century understanding of the role of the Messiah as a military conqueror/liberator. Jesus resisted fitting into this mold His entire life. At the very outset of His ministry, just after being baptized by John in the Jordan, Jesus spent a while in the wilderness sorting out His options. He was tempted with all the popular messianic expectations and rejected them all. But He wasn't finished with it. He was tempted with it again and again.

Once, through Peter, Jesus ran into the same temptation He met in the wilderness. Although Jesus tried constantly to get the Suffering Servant concept from Isaiah across as His chosen model for the Messiah, the people never heard it. In their minds, the Messiah was coming to relieve their misery. Thus, there could be no suffering around the Messiah. So that day at Caesarea-Philippi when Jesus "began to show his disciples that he must go to Jerusalem and suffer many things" (Matt. 16:21), it was completely antithetical to what the Jewish people believed to be true. Even though Jesus got the idea from their own Bible (Isa. 40—66), they couldn't hear it. When Jesus said, "Where misery is, there is the Messiah," it took more than "flesh and blood" to reveal that to the people (see Matt. 16:17).

It took a miracle called "resurrection" to do it, for it wasn't until a postresurrection appearance that "he opened their minds to understand the scriptures, and said to them, 'Thus it is written, that the Christ should suffer' " (Luke 24:45-46). When Jesus got angry at Peter and called him a devil, I believe He was getting a bit tired of people trying to tell Him how to live His life.

Jesus Felt Anger at Institutions

Jesus got angry at institutions. When He cleansed the Temple in Jerusalem Jesus was demonstrably angry (Matt. 21:12-14). He acted out His anger by causing a stampede in church and disrupting the Temple trade. This time His anger was focused at the most sacred structure in all Judaism. Why? Because it was no longer fit to hold the wine of pure religion (Mark 2:22). The Temple had become a barrier intended to exclude certain kinds of people, and this aggravated Jesus. He said to them, "Is it not written, 'My house shall be called a house of prayer for all the nations'? But you have made it a den of robbers" (Mark 11:17). This action had dangerous consequences for Jesus; according to the Gospel writers, it led to the cross. Jesus got angry when He saw some people mistreated in the name of God. That was an anger that was not sinful.

Jesus Felt Anger at God

I would also suggest that Jesus even felt anger at God. That too is a common human experience, and Jesus lived and died as the fullest of humans. I sense some anger at the cross. This time Jesus had pity for His mother and anger for His Father. To His mother, He said, "Woman, behold, your son!" Then He said to the disciple, "Behold, your mother!" And from that hour the disciple took her to his own home" (John 19:26-27). That's what He said to His mother.

To His Father, He seems to express anger. See it in one of the words from the cross which have come to be so ingrained in our thinking that they have taken on a stained-glass hue—too holy to be human. But it seems to be a cry of abandonment: "My God, my God, why hast thou forsaken me?" (Matt. 27:46). It was not too human to be holy. The bystanders thought Jesus was calling for Elijah to come to the rescue, but I believe for one brief moment on the cross, Jesus felt the anger of all who feel they are abandoned. Anger is a common consequence of estrangement, isolation, brokenness, and loneliness.

Too many people try to relate to God only with logic or reason. Not Jesus. Jesus included His feelings in His relationship with His Father. There was nothing sterile in that relationship. We don't have to worry about those who get angry at God. It's those who ignore God who really blow it. One way to do God in is to scratch God off the list of those to whom one will relate.[2] To be an atheist is one way of expressing anger toward God. Jesus was no atheist. Thus, He was honest and open with God about His anger, knowing that it would deepen the relationship. See how Jesus quickly resolved His anger at His Father. For it wasn't too long after the cry of abandonment that we hear, "Father, into thy hands I commit my spirit!" (Luke 23:46).

Jesus, who had no problem linking the Messiah with suffering, also linked anger with being human as a part of living and a part of dying. He recognized that sinning has to do with running away from our humanity. It has more to do with becoming separated from ourselves, others, and God.

God Prefers Us Hot

That's why in the last book of the Bible He's at it again, wishing we were hot [angry?] or cold (Rev. 3:15). *God prefers us hot.* Jesus is not afraid of our heated human emotions because He knows at least we are being real, and anger is a part of our being human.

We are children of God, created in God's image, so we must be who we are. "Be angry and sin not," as Paul advised. It is a part of you. Don't try to be something you are not. That would be pretentious, and we know how God feels about that. Our human feelings are a given. We cannot always control them. Sad things touch our grief. Funny things make us laugh. Maddening things make us mad. That is the way life is.

The issue is not *to be angry* or *not to be angry,* but how do we deal with the anger that is a part of us? In *One Flew Over the Cuckoo's Nest,* Patrick McMurphy was an angry man. He stayed in trouble because of it and wound up in a mental institution where he made so many waves that his anger was surgically removed by a frontal lobotomy. The film ended with McMurphy unable to feel anything. He could only lie flat on his back like a zombie.

How can being human like Jesus enable me to work through my anger? Our faith in Christ sets us free to be able to experience our anger, to try to seek the wisdom in its creation and then express it positively. This is important because if we don't do something constructive with our anger, it will do something destructive to us. Like William Blake's poem:

> I was angry with my friend;
> I told my wrath, my wrath did end.
> I was angry with my foe;
> I told it not, my wrath did grow.

Anger can be repressed, projected, and rationalized, but anger will not be denied. It becomes wrath on which the sun went down (see Eph. 4:26). This sets up barriers which block love or anything else until anger is ministered to.

It is important that we be angry. If we cannot be angry, we cannot love. Putting a damper on one part of our soul inevitably puts a damper on the other parts too. We can love in proportion to our ability to feel in general, and to feel and express our anger in particular. Putting a concrete lid on negative feelings will put a lid on our positive passions also, and we risk ending up like Patrick McMurphy with emotional lobotomies.

Those people who have meant the most to me in life and inspired me beyond myself have been the ones with the most complete souls. They could be incensed with anger and rage like a prophet over some injustice. They could feel, deep down in their bones, the grief of bereaved people in their sorrow. And they could get tickled inside out by the joy of a little child or the foolishness of a colleague. They have been the most beautiful people to me. Such a person was Jesus, who knew better than anybody the beauty and wisdom of being a whole person.

It is a lifelong challenge to be able to learn to express anger creatively. But to keep our anger from being destructive, we must become more aware of it. Let us ask ourselves: Where did the anger come from? How is it being expressed? What is the outcome? We can be angry and not sin if our anger is not rooted in selfish concerns, if it is expressed directly or shared in an appropriate setting, and if it is not destructive to persons. This kind of anger is not sin. Let us give heed to our anger, and under God do our best to "Be angry but do not sin." As the wise man put it long ago, "A man of great wrath will pay the penalty;/for if you deliver him, you will only have to do it again" (Prov. 19:19).

8

When You Feel Trapped

(Luke 4:16-30)

This is the story of two cities: more accurately, what Jesus did in these two cities, and what people of both cities let Him do. In this story, we learn something about being human like Jesus who knew what it was like to be trapped.

All spoke well of him, and wondered at the gracious words which proceeded out of his mouth; and they said, "Is not this Joseph's son?" And he said to them, "Doubtless you will quote to me this proverb, 'Physician, heal yourself; what we have heard you did at Capernaum, do here also in your own country.'" And he said, "Truly I say to you, no prophet is acceptable in his own country. But in truth, I tell you, there were many widows in Israel in the days of Elijah, when the heaven was shut up three years and six months, when there came a great famine over all the land; and Elijah was sent to none of them but only to Zarephath, in the land of Sidon, to a woman who was a widow. And there were many lepers in Israel in the time of the prophet Elisha; and one of them was cleansed, but only Naaman the Syrian." When they heard this, all in the synagogue were filled with wrath. And they rose up and put him out of the city, and led him to the brow of the hill on which their city was built, that they might throw him down headlong. But passing through the midst of them he went away (Luke 4:22-30).

The City of Nazareth

In this city, Jesus got off to a bad start. In His hometown of Nazareth, it began on the sabbath. In the synagogue He read from the Old Testament, and when He finished He took a seat and all got quiet. Jesus was showing how the Scriptures were being fulfilled in His own ministry. Then He anticipated their negative response to what He was doing. Strangely enough, it had something to do with what had happened in another city.

The Problem of Proverbs

Jesus said, "I know you are going to say to Me this proverb: 'Physician, heal Yourself.' " It's funny how folks always seem to come up with a proverb for everything, because anecdotes do come in handy. "Physician, heal Yourself." We've heard what You did over in Capernaum, but this is Nazareth. What are You going to do here? Can You accomplish in Nazareth what You did in Capernaum? (author's paraphrase).

Proverbs are frustrating.—I know what it feels like to be where Jesus found Himself being characterized in this context. "Doubtless you will quote to Me this proverb." Sometimes proverbs are amusing and they make us laugh. But most of the time proverbs are frustrating. Jesus sensed in advance that He might get a negative reaction in Nazareth.

There are a lot of proverbs that hang around church. Especially do we hear proverbs when people start talking about money. "We need a real stewardship effort this year. People need to be challenged in their commitment. The church programs are being presented and things seem to be happening. Expectation is in the air and, of course, that means the budget is going to be higher." And here come the proverbs: "We can't: What if ?" "But we need this publicity, so we can become better known in this city." And here comes the proverb: "Why, we've done without that for years: Why do we need it now?" Bring up the issue of a music minister, and we hear all kinds of proverbs! One says, "Let's do this," and here comes a proverb. Another says, "Let's do that instead"; more proverbs and more proverbs.

Jesus knew what was coming.—"Doubtless you will quote to me this proverb," so He said it first, beat them to the punch, and took the wind out of their sails. "Physician, heal yourself." Why not do for the Nazarenes what you did in Capernaum? But it isn't as easy as it sounds. Proverbs never are. It wasn't easy because Jesus was closer to the Nazarenes than He was to those in Capernaum. The people in Nazareth knew Him, and they knew where He lived. They had watched Him grow up among them. They said, "Is this not Joseph's son?" (v. 22). It is at this point that nearness, closeness, knowledge, or familiarity gives us problems. A prophet has trouble the closer he gets to home.

The Nazareth Complex

What is it about nearness that does this to us? What is it about the familiar that blinds us to its potential? Why does fun have to call for driving two-hundred miles away? Why does the best help available cost over fifty dollars an hour? This blindness to what is present within our own midst is what I call the Nazareth complex. Familiarity does us in. "We know him; that's Joseph and Mary's son, and you know about Mary. Everybody knows about her!"

Teeners have this Nazareth complex.—They won't listen to their parents. They won't listen to their teachers or their counselors—they only listen to each other! They primarily are swapping ignorance and experience when good help is there for the asking. Young adults know about the Nazareth complex too, thinking that some college degree or quick once-over at a new job qualifies them as experts to overturn everything which has been established for years. Older adults have it too, insisting that the world be the same as it was decades ago, trying to turn back the clock to "when we were the greatest."

We are all caught in the educational half-life.—This refers to the time that it takes for half of your training to be worthless. For a minister it's ten years. For a physician it's four, and for an astronaut it's six months. The point is that you have to keep on learning, and the older you get the harder the pace is to keep up. We need to realize that Jesus did not stay in Nazareth. He left His home town. To say He left puts it mildly, doesn't it? Luke tells us *how* He left. He actually got run out of town, and He never went back as far as we know. Instead, Jesus left Nazareth where He could do nothing productive, where He was seen as a failure, and He went elsewhere where He could work. Does it shock you to hear Matthew say (13:58) that even Jesus' power could not work everywhere—much less ours?

The City of Capernaum

It took me three years to relocate when I moved from my former pastorate to where I am serving today. I became convinced from within and without that I could be more effective at another place of service. I recall how *long* those three years seemed to be. It was a lonely pain because I couldn't share it with those closest to me. But on this side of the experience, it doesn't seem so long. When you cannot move, the minutes seem like light-years. When you see your gifts drying up and rejection becomes too familiar, it does something to your faith. That feeling of helplessness can cause your gifts to wither, but something can be done about it if we let Jesus be our model. Once again, Jesus is our Savior when we feel trapped. Don't we have to do as He did and take the initiative in finding a suitable place to serve? When I moved from the North to the South I exchanged a set of problems. I don't believe I have any less problems. I might have more. I don't know because I haven't counted.

But at least they are new problems! Some of the old ones that I had grown accustomed to just aren't here. Instead, I have others that have taken their place and some, I am sure, that will take some time to learn to deal with. But isn't that life's challenge? It's good for you and it's a change, at least, to swap problems. There is no heaven here; there is no state of perfection in this life, no free ride, no idyllic tranquillity. There are permanent tasks we have to live with wherever we go, and geography isn't a point with them. But I've learned that rotating my pain helps every now and then. Finding and knowing our gifts are essential, no matter where we are; and starting all over again after a little rest can be helpful.

When You Feel Trapped

What we are talking about here is the issue of entrapment. The attitudes like those in Nazareth can entrap you. They can catch you, grasp you, surround you, and taunt you at your hurting point of vulnerability. "Jesus, you think You are a Christian world doctor. Why, You can't even heal Yourself! We know who You are. Go ahead, 'Physician, heal Yourself.'" And Jesus replied at some length to that, talking about Elisha, one of their heroes, helping a foreign leper. But that didn't get through to them.

It was at that very point when they got mad at Him and tried to kill Him. Sometimes the worst thing you can do in "Nazareth" is to prove Nazareth wrong. You had better watch out who you prove wrong! Some folks will be thankful for it, but most will make you suffer for it because nobody likes to be trapped.

Must Nazareth entrap us? Must the help we could give in one place go wasted in another? Must pride keep us from admitting failure, from starting all over? Entrapment is hard to deal with, and there are times when we just can't seem to get out of Nazareth even though we want to get out. We are stuck. We are trapped in some Nazareth, marking time, being ineffective—maybe.

You Can't Run from Problems

Follow the ministry of Jesus and you will surely find that He had other times like this one in Nazareth. You see, Nazareth was no striking exception in a string of receptions elsewhere. Again, I emphasize we do not get rid of problems. The best we can do is to get a new set of problems to work on when the old ones have worked on us so long that we feel entrapped by them. And there is deliverance in that sense of turning it over. I am trying to get us to see how hard it is to minister in some places. Jesus had a tough time relating to some folks, and we should not be too bewildered if we find ourselves hindered physicians sometimes too. We all have our Capernaums where grace flows and somehow we do a mighty work. We all have our Nazareths where we can do none at all—where we just strike out. Even in the same place on the same day, we will have Capernaum times and Nazareth times. Call it inconsistency, contradiction, or hypocrisy; call it what you like. It's just a fact.

Take Care of Yourself

I think this is what made Jesus slip away for a few days of R&R. He knew the wisdom of withdrawal. People were always finding Him alone in deserts, in a boat, or buried in swarms of little children—in places doing things where any American savior worth his salt would not be. But Jesus needed those getaways. So do we. If things turn sour in Nazareth, why keep multiplying failure? Find a Capernaum and go there. Find some way to take care of your own needs.

But sometimes self is in Nazareth and we cannot leave. Why do we physicians have trouble healing ourselves? We have Bibles; we know how to pray. We have Christian friends. God is our Savior. Why do we get sick and cannot recover, tempted and cannot refuse, proud and can't be humble, angry and can't get calm? We are saved—but. We are the light of the world—but. We are a royal priesthood—but. We are workers together with Christ—but. Salt of the earth—but. "Physician, heal yourself." Bitter sarcasm! Bitter proverb!

The world has seen more than one saint save others but not save himself; or someone near be not saved while saving someone far away. What does that mean if not that each of us is our own worst problem? Each of us is our own most deadly enemy. Each of us is our own most difficult puzzle. "Physician, heal yourself "!

But Nazareth was hometown, and Jesus could do no mighty work there. But can't Jesus do everything? "All power is given unto me in heaven and in earth" (Matt. 28:18b, KJV). We like to hear that. But what good was that power in Nazareth? Why was Jesus stopped, stumped, roadblocked, and deadended? Dare I say *failure?* You and I know that word. Is that a Jesus word? Did He know it? Evidently so. There were people Jesus wanted to help but could not, things He longed to accomplish but did not, places He wanted to improve but would not—because the Nazarenes simply would not let Him. And neither would Jerusalem. I wonder: Will we?

Here is a dose of reality for a lot of dreamworld religion that is popular these days: "All things are possible" (Matt. 19:26). Yes, I've preached that gospel too, and I believed it when I did. But sooner or later we all get to Nazareth where "all things are possible" becomes more of a sought-for spirit than a sober expectation. And if you ever hear me speak it again sometime, that's what it will be: a sought-for spirit, never a constant, realizable thing. Nazareth is going to come to us, or us to it. Like Jesus, we may just grow up there. But it's going to be Nazareth. When you feel trapped, go over to Capernaum; keep on kicking. You may surprise yourself. Consider the response of the two frogs and decide for yourself which was the most productive.

It seems two young frogs, after a night of partying and carousing, were caught off guard and fell into a farmer's pail of fresh milk. Before the two frogs knew what had happened, they had been dumped into the milk can from the dairy truck and were on their way to certain doom inside the airtight container.

After kicking and swimming frantically against the tide of milk, one frog quietly resigned himself to his fate and quit kicking. He died peacefully.

But the second frog bravely kept on kicking with all his might. After a while he discovered that his frantic activity had churned up enough to butter to float him to the top of the milk can where he survived until the can was opened.

The moral of the story: When discouraged in your Christian walk, keep on keeping on. A few more "kicks" may "bring the butter."[1]

Now a word of hope. As dim as it seemed on that day that Jesus began His ministry—He got thrown out of church—but He had His Capernaums that followed immediately. Look at verse 31: "He went down to Capernaum, a city of Galilee. And he was teaching them on the sabbath; and they were astonished at his teaching." He found astonishment in Capernaum. He found faith in Samaria. He made wine in Cana. He dazzled the disciples with light on Mount Hermon. He sent out seventy and saw them return. He prayed in a garden, spoke with Nicodemus at night, helped Zacchaeus down from a sycamore tree in Jericho. It came back some days. That reminds me of another Scripture: "Let us not be weary in well-doing: for in due season we shall reap, if we faint not" (Gal. 6:9, KJV).

How can being human like Jesus make us better persons? It can teach us not to toss in the towel when we feel like giving up. Jesus didn't let His bad start prevent Him from serving God. Nazareth told Jesus *no.* "And he went down to Capernaum, . . . and they were astonished at his teaching." Perseverance is a quality that enables us to endure our Nazareths until we land in Capernaum someplace. Nothing worthwhile ever gets done without sticking to it. Let us learn from Jesus the secret to serving God: when one door closes in our face, God might be opening another door somewhere else.

9

When Forgiveness Is Hard

(Matt. 9:1-8)

I recall a popular song a few years ago called "Breaking Up Is Hard to Do." It revealed a truth about you and me. It was a song that told about how we break up and how we make up. We are always doing one or the other, aren't we? We are either making up or breaking up; on again, off again, coming and going. Which is easier? The song writer thought breaking up is hard to do. But I have learned that making up is just as difficult—and maybe even more so.

Which Is Easier?

Consider Jesus' statement in Matthew 9:5: "Which is easier, to say, 'Your sins are forgiven,' or to say, 'Rise and walk'?" Which is easier: forgiveness or healing? In verse 6 we will find the answer. Jesus eventually said, "Rise, take up your bed and go home." That could mean a physical act is sometimes easier to accomplish than one which involves human emotions. To heal a person is sometimes easier than forgiving a person. It is sometimes easier to take a scalpel, cut somebody open, and sew them back up than it is to forgive a person. Breaking up is hard. Making up is harder.

Does Jesus surprise you with this text? We normally assume that Jesus found it easy to forgive people, branding it into our minds with that classic statement on forgiveness: "Father, forgive them; for they know not what they do" (Luke 23:34). You would think that forgiveness was a snap with Jesus, that there was nothing to it, that it just kind of flowed spontaneously from His being. But Jesus knew how hard it is to deal with human emotions. "Which is easier," said He, "to forgive or to heal?" Obviously, in this text in Matthew's Gospel, it was easier to heal in the presence of a pharisaical spirit than it was to forgive.

Why It's Hard to Forgive

Why do you think Jesus asked that question? I can think of several reasons, and one was that *He took sin a lot more seriously than we do.* He was willing to die because of it. We live in a society that doesn't take sin nearly as seriously. We live in a society that condones our sinning, making heroes out of men who openly admit lying.[1] We frown on murder, stealing, or somebody who is lazy and won't work. But concerning sins of the spirit—the ones that also do us in—we make a mockery of those kinds of sins in our society. When we take evil seriously, it makes it hard to forgive. Turn on the television. Watch it and listen to what you hear. Look at all the violence and all the sexual sins that are made light of, condoned, and laughed at. Walk down streets in our cities and see the abuse, exploitation, and ruin of young women and the men that they seduce. If you hear people talking about forgiveness in a lighthearted manner, you can be sure they are not forgiving sins. They are only condoning them. Forgiveness is hard because it *does* matter. To condone sin is easy; to forgive it is hard.

I've seen different kinds of parenting, for instance. Many times when kids do wrong we say, "Well, it's no big deal; why are you overreacting? What's all the fuss about? Don't get so strung out." But parents ought to know better. Some parents have no moral depth, and you can tell the difference in who does and who doesn't by how angry they get. Some parents raise prodigal sons and daughters who wallow around in vice and come limping back home, and they condone their sins. They end up making more excuses than the kids themselves can concoct.

But other parents take evil seriously and would never do that.

They would grant forgiveness, but it would be a serious kind of forgiveness. They would not condone the evil. There would be a sense of outrage because of what was done, almost as if they had committed it themselves. They would have walked down the path of any hell and stood grief stricken at the door of that hell until their child came out. They would put themselves in their child's place; they would feel the burden of their child's guilt; they would forgive. But it would turn their hearts heavy and their hair gray. That's what forgiveness is like, and it's hard to forgive because we have egos. In order to forgive, our egos have to diminish. Forgiveness means self-substitution, and that is never easy. "Which is easier," Jesus said, "to heal or to forgive?"

Love Makes Forgiveness Hard

Another reason Jesus found forgiveness difficult is *because He loved people so much.* When you care about what happens to somebody, it's not easy to forgive when you see another person's sin hurting a person you love. If you never love, you don't have to worry about forgiveness at all. But if you do love, then realize that forgiveness is going to be hard to come by.

There are other places in the Gospels which indicate that forgiveness was hard for Jesus. He was severe toward the scribes and the Pharisees because they "devour widows' houses and for a pretense make long prayers" (Mark 12:40). Why do you think Jesus was so concerned about widows? Maybe it was because His own mother was a widow, and He knew firsthand the special plight of those who live alone. Moreover, He honored a widow for giving all she had. He dealt with a widow from Nain, and in a parable He pictured a widow pleading to an unjust judge. Jesus condemned the scribes and Pharisees; and when He did it, I can imagine His mother's face in the background, having her own house devoured.

When it gets personal like that, knowing the suffering of innocent people makes forgiveness hard to come by. Jesus was equally tough on the priest and the Levite in the story about the good Samaritan because they "passed by on the other side," neglecting to help someone who was in need. When you care about people the way Jesus did, it makes it hard to forgive because nobody ever took sin as seriously as Jesus. Jesus saw what it did to human beings. Yet, He still taught and practiced forgiveness. That is the miracle: that God has a merciful side. God does forgive, but we must never take it lightly. Which is easier, to heal or to forgive? It isn't forgiveness.

Forgiveness Removes Sin

Another thing we need to recognize is what happens when somebody gets forgiven—what takes place. Jesus knew we needed forgiveness because of what it does to people. But we must see what forgiveness does not do. It does not take away the fact that we have sinned. What has been done is done and cannot be undone. Nor does forgiveness remove the memory from our minds of what we did or what we had done to us. People tritely say, "Forgive and forget," but I can't do that. I cannot forget what happened to me. I cannot forget what happened to somebody I care about.

Neither does forgiveness take away the consequences of what we have done, nor does it take away the consequences of what we have had done to us. We just have to live with that. Forgiveness is an act of the moral imagination by means of which one person gives another person his or her life back again. Forgiveness is not an experience of having something to live down; it is the experience of finding someone to live with.

Forgiveness does one thing only: *it allows the reestablishing of old personal relationships that have been severed by our sin against each other.* Forgiveness reconciles people who are separated but who ought to be together. Although we cannot forgive and forget, I have a suggestion for something we can do that could help us to be human like Jesus.

Forgiveness Means to Forego

We can forgive and forego.—Everybody can do that. We can't forget it, but we can consciously forego it. I can think of several things that we can forego that might enable us to be more forgiving.

To be forgiving, we have got to be willing to forego our pain.—Some people develop a martyr complex, and they don't give up their pain without a fight. They like to hold on to it. They seem to take a vile kind of pleasure in poking around in their own woundedness, and thus keep their sore spots lanced. It also keeps alive the guilt of those who may have wounded us too. But mostly, when we hold on to our hurt *we* get to feel superior; we get to condescend, to look down our noses, being one up on the person who hurt us. This way we get the satisfaction of knowing that we are right and they are wrong. We take pleasure in our pain like this, and sometimes we hesitate to let it go. But to be a forgiving person, we must be willing to forego our pain.

We also must be willing to forego our power.—Nobody likes to be vulnerable or weak. We go to great lengths to keep from being this way. We struggle to stay in control. It is this element of power that makes forgiveness a tough business. Power is at the root of it. The one who has been offended suddenly is granted power. The offender seeks forgiveness, and the offended has the power to give it or not.

That's where the blame comes in. My, how we like to blame!—which is something else, by the way, that we are going to have to forego. We enjoy scapegoating other people. "It's not my fault," we say.

The referee came out during a church softball game and we had a little ruckus over on third base. He said to me, "What's going on?" and I said, "It all started when he hit me back!" Pointing our fingers at the other guy, you see! It's a game that we play quite well with each other. Eric Berne calls it: "See What You Made Me Do"![2] There is power in blaming, and most of us like the power that comes from scapegoating and keeping folks dangling in mid-air.

But real forgiveness restores the balance of power from one-upmanship to equality. It is mighty tempting to keep folks over a barrel, all strung out. Once we have tasted moral superiority, it's easy to get hooked on it. But for those who are big enough to forego their power, their blaming, their guilt trips, and their scape-goating, they are in on the secret of liberation. They are able to forgive. It is amazing how ailing relationships can be restored to health by these simple but sincere words: "Will you forgive me?"

Another thing we've got to forego to forgive is our pride.—Like the Pharisee who in arrogance prayed, "I thank thee that I am not like other men" (Luke 18:11), when we get offended, we have the problem of enlarged egos. The ego has to be reckoned with in this matter of forgiveness. In times when we have been wronged, our ego and our self-image become all-important—so important that we see through blinders.

Because so many folks are wronged so often in our kind of world, selfishness has become the tenor of our time. Experts call this "narcissism." The word comes from a Greek myth about a man named Narcissus who was in love with himself. Ego inflation is found in many areas of our modern life. We hear slogans like: "Do your own thing," "I want what I want when I want it"; then there is the familiar jingle: "Have it your way"—the exact oppo-site of Jesus' prayer in Gethsemane, "Not My way, but Your way." Getting our way becomes ultimate in any kind of disagreement. Many times in life we simply aren't going to get our way about things; it's unrealistic to think so. Jesus told a story of two men who went up to the Temple to pray—a Pharisee and a tax collec-tor. The Pharisee got in trouble in Jesus' story, not because he was insincere, but because he was sincere—and proud of it! We must we willing to forego that kind of pride if we are going to be forgiving people.

I get tickled at the children and their interpretations of what we do in worship. You should see their eyes as they come in and hear us singing these hymns with the organ playing. In a church I pastored in Indiana, we had a baptistry that was down in the floor behind the pulpit. We had to lift up part of the carpet to baptize in it. We had to get down in this hole. One morning we had baptism and this kid went home; her mother asked her what went on in church that day. She said, "We had baptism, and the preacher said a funny thing. He said, 'I baptize you in the name of the Father and the Son, and down in the hole you go!'" To her, it looked as if we put them down in the hole.

I heard a young child who misunderstood the big people when they recited the Lord's Prayer. Instead of "Forgive us our trespasses," he thought they said, "Forgive us our trash baskets, as we forgive those who put trash in our baskets." Really, it isn't far from the truth because most of us operate under the principle that it is easier to get forgiveness than it is to get permission. People are always going to be putting trash in our baskets. You are going to be hurt; you are going to be treated wrongly. There *ain't* no justice in this world! You are going to be discriminated against. You are going to be embarrassed; you are going to be angered and embittered. You will search for ways to retaliate, like Peter who asked, "Lord, how often shall my brother sin against me, and I forgive him?" (Matt. 18:21). Isn't that a good question? How many times have I got when I have to quit forgiving this turkey? Jesus said, "I do not say to you seven times, but seventy times seven" (v. 22). You see, seventy times seven means *always*. Forgiveness that is conditional like Peter's isn't forgiveness at all; it's just fair warning. We are better warners than we are forgivers.

Even more serious is the fact that we often put trash in God's basket. What does the cross mean if it doesn't mean this: forgiveness is costly. It cost God to forgive you and me, and that is true to life as I have known it. If you forego to forgive, it will cost you.

Just how much it will cost can be seen by the way Peter responded when he saw in the miraculous catch of fish the beauty and power of Jesus; Peter fell to his knees and cried, "Go, Lord, leave me, sinner that I am" (Luke 5:8, author's paraphrase). A person seeking forgiveness bad enough to kneel for it is one who realizes how truly tall a human being can stand. A kneeling person is a victor over pride, and one who has the courage to look above self to find oneself. A kneeling person is the only person who can honestly say, "I believe the forgiveness of sin is difficult to receive."

Let us not hesitate to kneel before God to find out what we have become, and who we might yet be. We need to kneel because we get tied up in knots by a chain of past mistakes, because we are dominated by what we have been instead of thoughts of what we might become. Let us kneel to receive fresh chances and God's grace to make good those chances.

So, making up is hard to do, but the truth is that it can be done—with God's grace and our not having to save face. We can be forgiving people like Jesus, but it is never easy; we will never be able to forgive and forget. We can, like Jesus, learn to forgive and forego. We can forego our pain, we can forego our power and our pointed fingers, and we can forego our pride. This involves difficult actions like repenting. That's what forgiveness is about. It involves confessing. It involves making up. When we do that, we have discovered the liberating secret.

10

When God Said No to Jesus

(Luke 22:39-46)

Sweating is a distinctly human function. Normally, we think of it as a result of work and toil. That's simple sweating. "No sweat" as some would put it. In Jesus' case, however, it had to do with inner conflict. Luke indicated that Jesus was "in an agony," so He was sweating like "great drops of blood falling to the ground" (Luke 22:44, KJV). That's some sweat! Anything that bothers Jesus that much needs to be examined more closely.

I have stood near the garden spot where this occurred. It is just across the valley outside the walls of Jerusalem on the Mount of Olives. Just being there one can see the gnarled old olive trees, some over two-thousand years old. The name *Gethsemane* means "wine press or oil press." It was an appropriate place for One to struggle under pressure.

There Jesus agonized with questions about life and death, success and failure, friends and foes, pain and pleasure, suffering and redemption. There was His struggle with the will of Another laid bare as no place else. It was a struggle by Jesus for His own sanity. He found Himself pressed in a conflict between human desire and divine will. The veil of the mystery of the God-man was momentarily lifted, and Jesus, the human, struggled to obey the will of God. In the garden we discover something about being human like Jesus.

You learn a lot about people by observing how they react to pressure. Here in Gethsemane, the soul and character of Jesus were laid bare for us to see. Here was a crisis so intense that its symptoms were not merely emotional but also physical. What caused the sweat? What Jesus really shrank from was not death as a painful experience or physical death at the hands of the Romans, but spiritual death and separation from His Father. He was not just afraid of the nails that would tear his flesh but the evil that would ravage His soul. Jesus did not only wince from the moment when His disciples would forsake Him but that dark hour next Friday when God would (Matt. 27:46). Who knows when a person comes to a point of thinking he faces more than he can possibly bear? But considering all that had happened to Jesus, I can understand the sweat.

He had started out in style, with the Wise Men bringing gifts from the East. But Joseph and Mary had spent that long ago because they were poor. Jesus preached to large crowds; He healed the sick and tried to train followers. The only writing He did was in the sand (John 8:6). He took no journeys beyond tiny Palestine. He received no recognition from organized religion. He left no sons or daughters and made few famous converts. His initial popularity in Galilee turned into opposition, which made even His faithful disciples susceptible to the temptation to give up.

Pressure

At this time Jesus was under incredible pressure. Everything was getting squeezed. Time was running out on the itinerant ministry of Jesus—still ambiguous, still threatened and hounded by John's skeptical question: "Are you he who is to come, or shall we look for another?" (Luke 7:19).

Think of the pressure that came from all the conflicting ideas of what was going on. The religious situation brought great pressure on Jesus. The old was dying and the new was struggling to be born. "You have heard that it was said to the men of old" was getting pushed out of the way by "I say to you." The "time had fully come;" the "hour" Jesus spoke of to His mother back at Cana had arrived; for better or worse, new wine had been poured into old wineskins, and they were about to burst. Pressure!

The Religious Leaders

The religious leaders believed Jesus was a heretic. He had the audacity to say that the real troublemakers were not the ignorant and poor but the intelligent and corrupt—people like the Pharisees themselves. After He cleansed the Temple and chased the money-changers away, Jesus had purged the oldest form of corruption: religion turned into making money. Yet for all their power, they were powerless: "The Pharisees then said to one another, 'You see that you can do nothing; look, the world has gone after him'" (John 12:19).

Messianic Expectations

The crowds in Jerusalem did go after Him on Palm Sunday but they didn't know why. Were they cheering a religious leader or a political messiah whose power had been proved a few days earlier by the raising of a dead man named Lazarus? Oh, they carried branches, but only because Rome would not allow spears. They were praising God, to be sure, but they also had in mind a king of Israel. Some no doubt remembered the prophet saying: "Behold, thy King cometh unto thee: . . . lowly, and riding upon an ass" (Zech. 9:9, KJV). But my hunch is the majority had Saul or David in mind. These messianic expectations put pressure on Jesus.

Conflicting expectations meant conflicting emotions and more pressure. The Pharisees were sullen, the crowds were ecstatic. But even greater was the distinction between Jesus and the people. They celebrated wildly, "Hosannah! Blessed is he who comes in the name of the Lord, even the King of Israel!" (John 12:13). The king was not smiling in approval. Instead, the king was crying: "When he drew near and saw the city he wept over it, saying, 'Would that even today you knew the things that make for peace! But now they are hid from your eyes'" (Luke 19:41-42). He was weeping for what would come upon those people who were cheering Him on: tomorrow, they would be shouting, "Crucify Him!"

Loneliness

The loneliness brought its own special kind of pressure and although there were people around, the garden was a lonely place. It's lonely when you want your closest friends around but realize also that they must keep their distance. Do you sense the paradox of desiring company but needing solitude? Why did Jesus take them along to begin with? And why did those three who meant the most stop a little farther than the rest, "about a stone's throw"? (Luke 22:41). When Jesus did finally kneel down to pray, He had friends all scattered out. Some were in Bethany. Others were nearer at the edge of the garden. And His closest friends were only a few olive trees away. But there was Jesus—all alone.

Perhaps they were there because Jesus wanted them there but not too close. Paradoxical situations like that create pressure. The desire for intimacy at the same time as distance underscores a fact about human beings: we can get only so close to others. Partners, yes, but no mergers. Some space must remain. Gethsemane teaches us that we can never overcome the space of separation.

Nevertheless, when we are in trouble, we want somebody with us. We don't necessarily want them to do anything, or even talk. We only want them to be there. Gethsemane was a lonely place.

What can we learn about being human like Jesus from His experience in the garden?

A Struggle for Insight

A struggle for insight in the presence of uncertainty is one thing we see. Jesus voiced something of the question that He was previously asked by John from behind prison bars: Is this the only way, or should I look for another? Surely Gethsemane was a place where Jesus struggled to understand what He was to do. When folks get in a crack like that, we can gather our most loyal friends around us and pray to God in their presence for guidance. I wonder how often people today do this when they find themselves in tough spots? Most of us fly by the seat of our pants, taking little time either to pray or to seek guidance in our problems. There are too many know-it-alls and too few like Jesus who seek to understand the complexities that lie ahead of them. The result is suffering.

Jesus wondered about the bitter cup before Him. Should He drink it or not? Jesus wasn't sure what to do. Ever been there? That's why Gethsemane has no address but our own. There in the garden, alternative wills completed with each having reasons and claims.

There was no magic in Gethsemane, only faith. Jesus prayed, "If thou art willing, remove this cup from me" (Luke 22:42). "Remove this cup" bared the humanness of Christ. He struggled with His own will. But there was that "if." What do you mean *if?* We are *ifs!* We don't want anymore *ifs,* nor any *maybes* or *yes-buts* or *on the other hands.* We want absolutes. We want magic formulas. Gethsemane is faith in action, but it brings out the sweat and blood. So "if thou art willing." The "thou" was not willing. Jesus was told no. The cup will not be removed, and He accepted God's will. When God says *no* to us, we can say *yes* to God. That's what Jesus did.

There is that *if.* But don't overlook the "nevertheless not my will, but thine, be done" (v. 42). That is not the acquiescence of a trapped and doomed man who despondently accepted the inevitable. Rather, it is a deep act of trust. In the end Jesus had to do what we must do sometimes, accept what we cannot fully understand. Jesus didn't just talk about God's will. For Him, God's will was not to be known but to be done. In the garden, Jesus recognized that the cross would terminate His work. But He also came to understand that it would germinate His work.

A Struggle to Live

A struggle to live and the fear that He might not live is something else we see in this account. Jesus did not want to die (see Het. 5:7-10). No one does who enjoys being alive. Jesus had a wholesome Jewish enjoyment for living. He relished His associations with others. He had a healthy zest for a tasty meal. He was no morose neurotic with death wishes. He did not welcome His demise anymore than anyone who is of sound mind and body. He was about thirty-three, and life was good for Him. Jesus had watched the sun set over the water and heard the laughter of little children. He had tasted the savory lamb at Passover and touched the grass in Galilee. So He naturally shrank from the death that loomed ahead for Him. Death, for Jesus, was the enemy, because Jesus had a strong will to live. That is the reason for the struggle.

I think there was some fear behind that sweat. That is why He had to force Himself to go on. There was nothing phony about Gethsemane or the One praying in it. Jesus was not acting as if it were make-believe. I think it is normal to be afraid in the face of death. But Jesus prayed not only that the cup would pass, but that God's will be done. And "remove this cup" is an appropriate prayer for the Christ or any Christian, for that matter, as long as we follow with that "nevertheless." This agony was real. The sweat was like blood drops.

The Courage to Obey

Now we come to the positive side, and this is also something that pertains to humanhood. For in the garden, along with the uncertainty and fear, we also see *a courageous willingness to obey*—a submission of One will to the Other. What Jesus struggled to understand, and the cup from which He hesitated to drink, He nevertheless drank to the bottom. That took guts.

Jesus weathered His severest storm thus far because of special resources He had acquired along the way to the garden. Resources,

I might add, that are also available to us to enable us to be better humans. What were they? Jesus' relationship with God won the victory in the garden, as He had earlier in the wilderness. Where did Jesus get such resolve? He prayed. Why did the disciples fail so miserably? They slept. "The spirit is willing but the flesh is weak" (Matt. 26:41). So Jesus advised, "Rise and pray that you may not enter into temptation" (Luke 22:46).

That means life's crises must be prepared for along the way, or ahead of time. When we stand face-to-face with our crises, hopefully they will find something already on the inside of us to resist and stand firm. Jesus didn't wait until it was too late. He had been preparing for this since the age of twelve at the Temple in Jerusalem (Luke 2:49). Jesus had run into temptation before and had conquered it in the Judean wilderness (Matt. 4:1-11). He had had a brush with death in His hometown of Nazareth that day He preached for the first time in His local synagogue (Luke 4:28-30). He had known disappointment: "After this many of his disciples drew back and no longer went about with him. Jesus said to the twelve, 'Do you also wish to go away?' " (John 6:66-67). All this happened *before* Jesus made His way to this solitary place to pray alone. Jesus brought all of this with Him to the garden.

When Judas arrived soon after Jesus uttered His "nevertheless," everybody panicked but Jesus. Peter cut off a soldier's ear and the rest ran away to hide. But not Jesus. Betraying, fighting, running, and hiding were reserved for those who slept while Jesus prayed.

Jesus' experience in the garden shows us that we don't always get our wishes. When God turns us down, it is natural to suppose that God doesn't care. God says no to us *not* because He doesn't care about us, but precisely because He *does* care and has better plans for us. Through God's personal involvement in our everyday lives, seemingly negative experiences become positive opportunities for growth and development.

Jesus learned how to receive a firm no in answer to His prayers, yet He also learned to be grateful for it. Upon reflecting over God's will for His life, Jesus realized that He was fulfilling a divine purpose; therefore, His disappointment and hardship were justified.

This is how Jesus helps us to be human. Today, Christians can learn to accept God's negative responses by realizing that we, too, are part of God's plan and have a definite purpose to carry out. Though we may not always understand God's workings in our lives, we can carry on with confidence and joy because of God's undying promise of love and concern embodied in Jesus Christ.

The prayer of an unknown Confederate soldier hints at what Gethsemane can mean for us:

> I asked God for strength, that I might achieve;
> I was made weak, that I might learn to humbly obey.
> I asked for health, that I might do greater things;
> I was given infirmity, that I might do better things.
> I asked for riches, that I might be happy;
> I was given poverty, that I might be wise.
> I asked for power, that I might have the praise of men;
> I was given weakness, that I might feel the need of God.
> I asked for all things, that I might enjoy life;
> I was given life, that I might enjoy all things.
> I got nothing that I asked for—but everything I had hoped for.
> Almost despite myself, my unspoken prayers were answered.
> I am, among all men, most richly blest.

Christ did not agonize in Gethsemane so we could have a "deep religious mood." His struggle demands that we struggle. We have all been given the gift of living one life and dying one death. When the time comes for us to walk our lonesome valleys, let us take heart in the fact that we do not have to walk them by ourselves. The life-giving Lord is there to join us in the pilgrimage through the gardens and the valleys, and to sweat along with us.

11

When God Refused to Tell Jesus Why

(Matt. 27:46)

Perhaps you heard about the grandson who loved his grandmother so much he wanted to marry her. He came and announced his decision to his father one day: "I am going to marry Grandma." The best his father could answer was, "Well, no; you can't do that. It's not allowed." "Why not?" replied the boy, somewhat irritated. "You married *my* mother. Why can't I marry *your* mother?"[1]

Children aren't the only ones who ask unanswerable questions. Philosophers can. Saints can. Jesus did. Listen to it. "My God, my God, why hast thou forsaken me?" (Matt. 27:46). Some questions are not to be answered, but only to be lived with and, in Jesus' case, died with.

This is a genuine question that came from Jesus' lips. It has to be because it would have embarrassed the early church. It could not have been invented by them. No, the question rings with clumsy authenticity. It is one they would have preferred to forget. Remembering it was like admitting that apple pie is not American. It was something Jesus' followers wouldn't naturally attribute to Him.

Yet, there it is: "My God, my God, why hast thou forsaken me?" In the entire Bible there is no other question so difficult to explain. I am certainly not equipped to explain it. But I have lived long enough to have something to say about it.

When I walked through the streets of Jerusalem, pondering the events of the last week of Jesus' life, in the middle of which stands the cross, it struck me that the account of the events associated with the cross of Christ take up nearly a third of the story in the Gospels. The evangelists seem to be saying, "We've told you the kind of person Jesus was, some of the things He said, and some of the things He did. Now let us tell you what they did to Him during that last week in Jerusalem."

And with that, they turn completely to the passion; somehow, the early Christians found the heart of the good news in it. This has never been easy for the world to understand. "For the word of the cross is folly to those who are perishing, but to us who are being saved it is the power of God" (1 Cor. 1:18). Nothing like it has happened before or since. Consider some facts about it.

Jesus Died

No other religion purposes a Savior to us who was insulted, attacked, betrayed, tortured, and executed. We are standing in the presence of deep mystery here. The fact is: God's Son died! How could God's Son die? Death is for humans, not Christ. Certainly we must recognize that there was more to God than what we experienced in Jesus of Nazareth, but all I know is that on Calvary's cross there was only one Person, and that Person died. That Person I believe to have been the Son of God. If there is one mystery that's harder to accept than "Christ was born," it is the baffling puzzle: "Christ died." Some people have trouble accepting a Messiah who is born, who suffers, who dies, and is buried. That Messiah is too human to suit them. But if we'll let Jesus be who He is, there's glory in it too.

Anytime a dramatic meeting of good and evil such as the crucifixion of Christ takes place in history, it gets clothed in song. People write poems about it and paint pictures of it. It becomes the topic of preaching in untold numbers of churches. One thing happens as a result of that: people line up and take sides, one way or the other. The brighter Jesus becomes, the uglier those become who put Him to death. The danger of that is, we distance ourselves from those who did the killing. But we were there too. Our sins were there. The same sins that put Jesus to death are quite familiar to us all.

We were there in the blindness of the religious leaders who could not see a larger truth. We were there in the selfishness of the money changers, who did not want the profitable traffic in the Temple courts disturbed. We were there in the disloyalty of Judas, who cared more for himself than for Jesus. Pilate represents us well. His political shrewdness made him try to free Jesus, but he washed his hands upon finding the cost too high. The crowd's emotionalism is familiar to us, stirred by propaganda to cry for something for which they were not sure. The fear of the disciples, who ran away leaving Jesus by Himself, is not foreign to us. We were there.

Many were there, but *Jesus still died a lonely death.* His nation rejected Him as a traitor. Some of His religion considered Him to be a heretic. The Roman soldiers spit on Him. His friends abandoned Him. The crowd jeered at Him. Jesus was alone, until His heart broke out into one of the most desolate cries: "My God, my God, why hast thou forsaken me?" (Matt. 27:46). We did that to Christ. While we were there in our sins, no one was there to support. When Jesus asked God why, He got no answer but silence, made even more stark by the darkness at noon (Matt. 27:45).

We were there because we still prefer people like Jesus better dead than alive. For when they've passed on, with or without our assistance, and we are enjoying the benefits of their commitments, we build monuments to them and set holidays in their name.

But after two thousand years, the world is not rid of Him yet! There were a few folks in Jerusalem who refused to take part in Jesus' crucifixion. There was Nicodemus, a religious man, who would not; Joseph of Arimathea, a businessman and member of the Sanhedrin, who would not; and a tiny group of females, who passionately adored Him, who would not. Would we?

I'm not sure beyond a reasonable doubt what I would have done that day the guards led the bearded young religious dissenter before the judgment seat of Pilate. As far as society was concerned, here was a Man who had absolutely nothing going for Him. He wouldn't comply—in the view of some—with the accepted religious standards. He owned no property. He had no regular mailing address, no visible source of income. He made people uneasy by what He did and said. He appealed primarily to the disadvantaged and the poor. I would like to think I would not have taken up the chant: "Crucify! Crucify!" But I don't know.

Three people were crucified on Calvary—two because they were too bad, one because He was too good. When somebody comes along and knocks the religious props out from under us, the business props and the political props, no wonder they crucified Him!

Jesus Suffered

There was suffering in the cross. That confounds us because we are used to seeing God as all-powerful. That's why folks have power, so they won't have to suffer. Yet, God suffers because He loves us. Love suffers. Love is vulnerable. Love bears all things. God does not look out for number one. God is not concerned with security. God does not calculate and say, "Careful now; this may lead to suffering." God lays the glory aside and enters our world of sweat and tears and allows His Son to be trampled on.

Jesus really suffered great pain. The crown on His head was plaited with real thorns. The spit was warm on His face. A tough whip took the flesh off His back. Sharp nails pierced His hands and feet. The blood spattering upon the earth was His. "Into thy hands I commit my spirit!" was really His last breath. Little wonder then that Jesus asked God why. "Why are you allowing this cruelty to happen to Me?"

But silence was the only reply. Ever been there? Jesus knows what that's like. Ever wanted answers to difficult problems? Jesus did too. What did you do? What did Jesus do? He trusted God anyway!

If Jesus' humanity showed in Gethsemane, it also showed from the cross, in the several human requests. He got thirsty. He asked why. Nevertheless, Jesus remained in control. The garden experience carried Him to the point of commitment, so He was able to say, "Not my will, but thine, be done." The cross became more than a simple tragedy; it took on deep meaning. Jesus said, "Father, forgive them; for they know not what they do." And "Into thy hands I commend my spirit" (KJV). In the midst of suffering He never veered from obedience to His mission of love. He showed us that this is the way God is, no matter what. God's nature is that of loving and caring. Not even crosses, with their terrible suffering, can stop that.

It is on the cross that we see Someone who made sense out of suffering. We don't see only death. We see life. We see Someone not having His questions answered and yet finding meaning in what was happening to Him.

Jesus Failed

Jesus wept, struggled and—here—He failed. So we see what we can do when we fail. Jesus failed in His hometown synagogue, so He went to Capernaum. He wept beside Lazarus's tomb, so He called him forth from the grave. He struggled against God in Gethsemane, but He said "nevertheless." He failed on Palm Sunday as He swung "triumphantly" around Olivet's brow, the crowd shouting "Hosannah!" at Him. By Friday, they were yelling "Crucify!" He appeared to have failed.

In the City of David, Jesus had appealed for a reform of religion, and the leaders of the people answered in Pilate's court, "Away with him" (John 19:15). He had failed. His disciples were entrusted with becoming the nucleus of the kingdom of God, but one betrayed Him, another denied Him, and they all ran away. He had failed. Jesus was opposed to violence as a method of change. The religious leaders accused Him of trying to usurp Caesar, and Rome crucified Him. He had failed—not just tiny failures, but colossal, total, and complete washouts. That Friday, Pilate, the religious leaders and all of Jerusalem, including His own disciples, thought Jesus was done for. "But Peter followed him at a distance, as far as the courtyard of the high priest, and going inside he sat with the guards *to see the end*" (Matt. 26:58, author's italics). Was it the end or only the beginning? Was it a colossal failure or an amazing victory?

Jesus Won

It was both. Jesus did fail, and yet—and yet—He won! As badly as He lost, it made the victory all the more stunning. For in losing, He won. Now we know what He meant when He said, "For whoever would save his life will lose it" (Mark 8:35); what the writer of Hebrews meant when he wrote, "For it was fitting that he, for whom and by whom all things exist, in bringing many sons to glory, should make the pioneer of their salvation perfect through suffering" (Heb. 2:10).

Here is the mystery: we don't have to wait for the resurrection to achieve the victory. It came on the cross. For there we see the most powerful force in the moral history of humanity—*vicarious self-sacrifice.* The life given by that One on the cross has done more to change men and women than any power on earth, the power of love. Jesus loved His way into our hearts by showing us that where there is power, there can be no love. And where there is love, there is no need for power.

Jesus Died for Us

Jesus cared enough about the world to die for it. As Paul put it, "[Christ] loved me and gave himself for me" (Gal. 2:20). Jesus did not die for the multitudes of faceless, nameless people. He died for you and me. He died for Judas as well as John, for Mary of Magdala as well as Mary of Nazareth. He died for both thieves who were crucified with Him, even for the bandit who kept cursing Him. He died for those who put Him to death. And He died obeying the will of His Father, who refused to tell Him why! So, the most terrible defeat of all time has become the most glorious victory of all time.

For myself, at least, I am glad things like this can happen. I know a lot more about failure than victory. *If the future belonged to the things that seem to succeed,* we, of all people, would be most miserable.

At a funeral I attended once, I found myself in the procession to the cemetery jammed between a Mercedes in front of me and a Jaguar behind me in my Ford Fiesta. Those driving the expensive automobiles seemed so successful, but that was only outward. I wouldn't trade places with either of them.

A television evangelist's empire seemed so successful, but that was outward success. Inside was corruption and behavior that has been an embarrassment to all Christianity. Things that seem to be succeeding aren't always so.

The church where I am pastor is located in the inner city of Birmingham. Outwardly, it seems so small and insignificant. It goes unnoticed and most people don't even realize it is a church. By our society's standards, we have all the earmarks of failure. We appeal to minorities and people who would not attend a regular church. We don't even have a steeple on our building, but at least it's paid for.

But, thank God, there is a force in this world deeper and *stronger than the things that succeed,* namely, the things that fail! Things that are everlastingly right—that honorably and sacrificially fail!—*they* are the strongest forces in the world.

I need to see Jesus asking that question "Why?" and not getting it answered, for I find myself in His shoes more often than not. I need to see Jesus fail and, in failing, succeed. For I have been tempted to give up the struggle, but always that Figure of this Man nailed to the cross sends me back to take up my task again. Can you believe it? The One whose hands are pierced with nail holes still holds the future in His grasp, while those with the hammer and swords hold nothing!

No illustration can compare with this truth, but perhaps this can illuminate. One of the most moving experiences of my life occurred when I was a five-year-old child. A terrible tragedy happened as my grandfather's car was blown to smithereens by some coward who was afraid to look him in the eye. I'm confident the one who wired the nitro to the motor didn't think a five-year-old boy would be in the car when it exploded, or perhaps he didn't even care about that.

All I know is: I was there. And because of it, I almost was not. But here I am now, still alive and kicking. Miraculously, I somehow survived the blast, the shock, the shrapnel in my body, and the trauma of the tragedy. Somebody blew up my grandfather and mangled my tiny body.

What kind of meaning would I attach to it? In fact, my Christian calling came about as a direct result of this very event. What had been the worst experience of my young life to that time actually was used of God to call me into the ministry. For one woman, Mrs. Helen Haskins, a dedicated Sunday School teacher, interpreted that event when I went back to church. There I stood, wrapped in bandages, wondering about it all, and Mrs. Haskins said to me: "Don't you worry, Danny boy; God's got something very special for you to do, or He wouldn't have let you live through that accident." I never forgot that word to this day. I remember that experience more than I remember the explosion. The joy of being called into the ministry by far overrides the pain and the disfigured left hand.

For a while, it looked as though vengeance was the victor back in 1947. But that was in the past. The future does not always belong to things that succeed. It didn't look too good for the Christian movement the day Christ died. But from that hideous event came the salvation of the world!

Jesus' Death Gave Me Life

By trusting in Christ, we can have life. Jesus' death somehow gives me life. This is not to deny that the entire Christ event—the birth, life, death, and resurrection of Jesus—is not equally life-giving. But it is to stress the centerpiece of the Christian drama: the cross. We're thinking of the death of our Lord now. Without Jesus' death, I would be dead. I mean by that, I would be without faith in God, without hope, without love. Without things like that, I may as well be dead. I may as well have died in the explosion back in 1947. Just get me an expensive car and forget it.

Most People Don't Care

But faith in Christ is not automatic. The Christ on the cross has to touch my life personally, individually. Without an active involvement in the body of Christ, my faith cannot survive for long. The church can survive many things—hatred, sin, television corruption, even persecution. But what imperils the church more than anything else is apathy by part of its members.

Who gets turned on by Jesus Christ anymore? Let a rock group come to town and people will camp out on the sidewalks, waiting to buy a ticket. Let our favorite college team lose a football game and the local river will flood with our tears. A sexy movie star shows off her body on a videocassette and men will slobber all over themselves. But God's Son dies on a cross for you and me, and . . . business as usual. We keep on tossing Frisbees at 3:00 PM.

I am challenging each of you to make Jesus Christ vital in your life. You may not be told the answer to your "whys," but live your life anyway. *The future doesn't always belong to things that succeed.*

Sometimes, to fail is the best way to succeed. Jesus said, "Unless a grain of wheat falls into the earth and dies, it remains alone; but if it dies, it bears much fruit" (John 12:24). So they put Jesus to death on the cross, thinking they were done with Him. What they didn't realize was the power of what one life can do that gets into people's hearts by caring enough to die for them. That is a power that the greatest powers on earth cannot touch.

That is why the cross of Christ continues to fascinate men and women in our own time. Our lives, like Jesus' life, are enigmas too. It takes an enigma to know an enigma. Life is mysterious and the cross tells it like it is for us. The cross reveals men and women at their worst. And yet, God uses it to awaken faith in us at our best.

You may never get the answer to your "whys." Life is so enigmatic that there may not *be* any one answer. Jesus didn't get any answers from God that Friday. But what you can get is the strength to carry on anyway. You can get a reason to live and, if need be, to die. You can get hope for your tomorrows.

What we must never do is to allow the cross to be wasted on us. Consider this parable. Once a group of people built a lighthouse to save people from the raging seas. Everyone who joined the group knew their commitment was to go out and rescue people in peril. But, after a while, they decided there was no reason for *all* of them to risk their lives. Some of them should staff the lighthouse. After more time, they decided they should all stay home and keep the light bright so people in danger could find their own way.

After more time passed, the group was not quite sure they even wanted bedraggled people dripping all over the carpet, so they dimmed the light a little. After an even longer time, they decided they needed a new carpet; maybe even an elevator would be nice. When the light went out, nobody noticed. And after another long while, someone quietly changed the sign outside from "lighthouse" to "clubhouse."

Let me press the point. If, as individuals, we are not integrating suffering and commitment into a productive part of our lives, the cross was wasted on us. If, as a church, we exist for ourselves only, we may be nice people and we may even do nice things for one another, but we are not a church of Jesus Christ. For God's sake and your own, don't let the cross be wasted on you!

12
When God Said No to Death

(Matt. 28:5-7)

God speaks in the strangest places—like burning bushes,
through Balaam's ass, a manger in Bethlehem, and a borrowed
tomb, to name a few. Sometimes God's eloquence comes from the
sound of silence. God's purpose concerning us is so vast, sometimes it can be fulfilled in no other way.

There are times when love must say *no*. On Easter, God said *no*
to death. Who would expect such good news to come from a
graveyard? One man who was forced out of Germany by the
Nazis, was a part of the Nuremberg war trials. He told about a
witness who lived for a time in a Jewish graveyard in Poland. It
was the only place he could live to escape the gas chamber.

The man wrote a poem during this time about a description of
a birth that took place in the graveyard. A woman gave birth to
a son and the eighty-year-old gravedigger assisted in the birth
process. When the newborn child uttered his first cry, the man
prayed: "Great God, has [sic] thou finally sent the Messiah to us?
For who else than the Messiah himself can be born in a grave?"[1]

Only God can bring life out of death. This is what Jesus did
during His life. On more than one occasion, Jesus reached into a
grave to bring back those who had died. He raised Jairus's daugh-
ter, the son of a widow from Nain, and his friend Lazarus of
Bethany. But these were resuscitations, for they all died again. In
these cases, Jesus was restoring life and only postponing death.

However, on Easter, God said a graphic *no* to death once and for all. He said it from a graveyard. It did not occur on the banks of the Jordan, on Mount Sinai, or on the busy streets of Jerusalem but, of all places, a lonely graveyard.

In my visit to Israel, the place that meant the most to me was the garden tomb, north of the Damascus Gate. I am aware that the best archaeological evidence indicates the Church of the Holy Sepulchre is the more likely spot for the actual occurrence. Nevertheless, the garden tomb looks like the place I imagined the resurrection to have occurred. It is a quiet garden that reminded me of John's description: "Now in the place where he was crucified there was a garden" (John 19:41). I was awestruck by what I saw. The huge stone was rolled away from the door, hewn out of solid rock. When I looked into the tomb, I felt like Peter and John must have felt for the very first time. Nobody had to tell me to be quiet as they did in the churches. Who could speak in such a place? If anyone spoke at all, it was in the form of a whisper.

I also saw the incongruity of John's statement about crosses and gardens. Significant religious events have occurred in gardens. The Bible begins in a garden called Eden, where the first pair made a foolish choice. Jesus committed Himself to the will of God in the garden of Gethsemane. And finally, He was buried and raised from the dead in a garden tomb.

But John's statement about the garden has a cross nearby. The incongruity is striking. Where flowers bloom and fill the air with fragrance, the greatest tragedy of history took place. Christ was crucified. But there also is a kind of appropriateness to it. The scene of death also was the scene of newness. Wherever the cross has been planted in the soil of human life, it seems to also grow a garden.

Jesus was mistaken for a gardener by Mary on Easter morning. There is a deep truth in this error. Christ is the true Gardener of human beings and whenever we have had the courage to live by the principle of the cross, flowers of repentance, roses of love, and lilies of service bloom. Wherever there is a cross, there will be a garden nearby.

Good news coming out of a graveyard seems strange, but Christianity is a strange faith. It is belief in a God whose greatness is beyond human comprehension. He is concerned about us so much that God became one with us and one of us to redeem us.

Isn't it also unusual that when God became one of us, He was born in a stable to poor parents and an oppressed people in one of the smallest countries in the world? When He was born, angels serenaded no high priests or world rulers but lowly shepherds.

Furthermore, Jesus grew up and associated with fishermen, tax collectors, prostitutes, and lower-class people. He rode into Jerusalem on a donkey, not in a chariot, and was greeted with palms, not trumpets. His "army" was not made up of trained soldiers but ordinary men and women.

Although He could have called ten thousand angels, He allowed Himself to be abused, judged, and crucified between two thieves. So when we consider the strangeness of the Christian faith anyway, is it so unusual after all that the best news of our Lord came from a graveyard? It was from the graveyard that God said no to death. This is incredibly good news from an unlikely place. What was the news in more detail?

"Do Not Be Afraid"

The first thing the women heard from the tomb was, "Do not be afraid" (Matt. 28:5). After an event of the magnitude of the resurrection, we might expect Jesus to provide us with a lengthy discourse on the afterlife. Instead, after greeting His disciples, He told them, "Do not be afraid" (Matt. 28:10). It was not "be of good cheer" (Matt. 9:2d, KJV), but, "Be not afraid" (KJV). So Easter becomes a commentary on John's words, "There is no fear in love, for perfect love casts out fear" (1 John 4:18). God lives and watches over His own. Therefore, Christ can enable us to be fully human. We need fear no power, force, or opposition; no sickness, circumstance, or condition; no person or principality. Fear not! God has said *no* to death.

Jesus knew what He was doing by speaking to our fear. Fear was all over the graveyard. The guards were trembling "like dead men" (v. 4). The women were filled with "fear and great joy" (v. 8). Jesus told His disciples, "Do not be afraid" (v. 10).

Fear was everywhere because something brand new had happened. We're not talking resuscitation now, but resurrection from the dead. This is not immortality of the soul, but the eternality of God. Nothing makes us more fearful than the unknown, the new and, in some cases, the different. Anytime we don't know what lies ahead, we become apprehensive.

And with the new comes risk. Not even Christians like risk, and sometimes it seems *especially* not Christians. More often than not, we bury our talents, opportunity, time, or trust given to us, and we do it not because we are lazy but because we like to hang onto a sure thing.

We feel more comfortable with what we have, nicely broken in—the old way of doing things, believing things, or thinking thoughts. Don't most of us regard a new thing as a nuisance or a threat? But the old is constantly being displaced by the new; and at no time does this hurt more than when the old is not a thing but a person, and the person is I.

"Don't be afraid," Jesus tells us. We can have confidence that can tide us over times of ending and beginning. We need not fear about falling off the edge. We will never catch up with the horizon. Why should we fear whatever truth we may find? For truth is always God's truth.

The passing of time, the coming and going, the rising and falling, the waxing and waning, the dying and rising, surely deserves better than our fear. These things deserve what we have and yet never quite seem to see—Jesus our Lord, standing at the empty tomb telling His children, "Don't be afraid."

"He Is Not Here: for He Is Risen"

The second piece of good news the women heard from the graveyard was, "He is not here: for he is risen" (Matt. 28:6, KJV). That is certainly good news. Jesus was not resuscitated to die again, but resurrected to live evermore.

Lies were told about Jesus, but they could not hold Him down. Jesus was hated, but hate couldn't do Him in. His resurrection was considered a "fraud" by some (Matt. 27:64), but He arose anyway. He was persecuted, slandered, and in the end executed, but not even death could hold Him down. He is risen!

Because He lives, so can we. Because He lives, truth lives, hope endures, love conquers, and integrity is justified. Because He lives, we can live too. "Therefore, if any one is in Christ, he is a new creation; the old has passed away, behold, the new has come" (2 Cor. 5:17). He is risen, to put love in our hearts, decent thoughts in our minds, and steel in our backbones. And that's the difference Jesus Christ can make in our lives.

"He Goes Before You"

The third thing the women heard was, "Then go quickly and tell his disciples that he has risen from the dead, and behold, *he is going before you* to Galilee; there you will see him" (Matt. 28:7, author's italics).

Jesus was always going *before* people. For Him there was always some promised land to go to. From the beginning when, mother like, Mary tried to keep Him on too tight a leash, her inquisitive Adolescent said, "Did you not know that I must be in my Father's house?" (Luke 2:49). "I cannot be held in childhood. I must forge ahead and move on to claim My destiny" (author's paraphrase).

Listen to the first words of His public ministry, alive with promise: "The time is fulfilled, and the kingdom of God is at hand; repent, and believe in the gospel" (Mark 1:15). "Something better than we have ever known is on the way, just ahead of us. Let us reach out and claim it" (author's paraphrase).

Jesus was always going before them, anticipating what was coming more than regretting what was going. Simon Peter tried to turn Him around at Caesarea-Philippi, but "his face was set toward Jerusalem" (Luke 9:53).

The early church understood what it meant for Jesus to "go before them," as the writer of Hebrews put it: "For the joy that was set before him [he] endured the cross, despising the shame, and is set down at the right hand of God [the Father]" (Heb. 12:2, KJV).

But it took Easter to make sense of it. He arose, still going before them, establishing light on the other side of the darkness of death and opened up the possibility for endless maturing toward the promise of God.

Wasn't the sin of Lot's wife a refusal to look forward to what was coming before her? Rather, she looked backward to what was going away. And with profound symbolic insight, the writer of Genesis said she turned into "a pillar of salt" (Gen. 19:26), as will all like her who keep looking back.

How different was Jesus. Said He, "No one who puts his hand to the plow and looks back is fit for the kingdom of God" (Luke 9:62). He is always going before us—out in front, leading the way, pioneering the faith, and calling us to follow. Our challenge is to be open enough to look for the blessing in the new rather than lament the passing of the old. Can we receive the new gifts that God gives us each day and not make idols out of them? Can I learn to let certain things go when the time comes in the confidence that new gifts of greater value may be coming?

Christ goes before us even now, in our many different directions, to smooth the rough, make straight the crooked, exalt the valleys, and level off the mountains.

Think of it. Our greatest discovery in all history occurred in a graveyard! Humankind's greatest discovery was not when we learned that the earth revolved around the sun, how to harness and channel the power of electricity, or split the atom. It didn't take place in a college or a laboratory. Our greatest discovery came when a few women, Easter's unlikely reporters, went to a graveyard expecting to anoint the dead body of a Man they discovered to be the living Lord!

The greatest battle that humanity ever fought was not at Waterloo, Gettysburg, or Pearl Harbor. Our greatest battle was fought in a lonely graveyard when Jesus Christ took on the power of death and won! Easter has less to do with one Person's escape from the grave than with the victory of powerless love over loveless power.

The greatest pronouncement that was ever made to men and women did not come from Caesar's household, the Reichstag in Berlin, or the Oval Office in Washington. It came from a graveyard when God said *no* to death through the messenger who spoke to the women,

> Do not be afraid; for I know that you seek Jesus who was crucified. He is not here; for he has risen, as he said. Come, see the place where he lay. Then go quickly and tell his disciples that he has risen from the dead, and behold, he is going before you to Galilee; there you will see him (Matt. 28:5-7).

That ought to have an impact on our lives if He lives in us. We need no longer be an insoluble problem to ourselves. In Jesus Christ, what it means to be a human is defined, declared, and demonstrated. In Him we learn at least that, although we may be brought to nothing, we cannot be reduced to nothing. "Thanks be to God, who gives us the victory through our Lord Jesus Christ" (1 Cor. 15:57).

Whatever else you may say about it, something happened on that first Easter day. No one tried to explain it. People just described their own experiences. The crucifixion shocked everyone. But while they were in an incredible state of shock, they became aware that Jesus was no longer dead. At the tomb, along the road, and by the sea, people who believed in Him became aware that their Friend was still alive. He was not dead. He lived.

Jesus is not dead when His Spirit stretches across centuries and touches those who submit themselves to each other and to Him. Jesus is not dead when through Him persons discover their own potential and begin to live up to it.

The question is: Do you and I have anything to look forward to? Yes, if we consider this: Jesus made it as a Man who lived, died, and rose, and if the Spirit that gave life to Him is still around, we certainly have something to look forward to! It is as though Jesus were saying, "I made it, so can you!" If that is the case—as I believe it is—then His life does matter, and ours does. That is something to look forward to.

"Why do you stand looking into heaven?" the disciples were asked once the risen Christ disappeared from their sight (Acts 1:11). In other words, they were not to remain dumbly staring off into space, because the resurrection was not the end but the beginning.

There was only one thing different about the world after Easter morning, and that was the existence of the church. Everything else was the same. Pilate crawled out of the same bed. The same shops in Jerusalem displayed their wares for all to see. And yet, everything had changed.

A little group of people were gathering. The women were telling their experiences. Jesus stood in the midst of them and they worshiped as the community of the resurrection; the Sunday people who were formed by a surprise and who are still willing to be surprised, reformed, and re-created. Their mission was to be a resurrected community, and to invite all to participate in the surprise of a God who is One of us, yet far beyond us.

We are simply those who have heard what the women said that first Easter morning and have experienced the presence of Christ for ourselves, standing among us on Sunday, with us. It can be said of us, like those first Easter people, "They worshiped him; but some doubted" (Matt. 28:17).

Every time we gather, some worship, some are afraid, and some doubt. Then comes Jesus to stand among us and say:

> All authority in heaven and on earth has been given to me. Go therefore and make disciples of all nations, baptizing them in the name of the Father and of the Son and of the Holy Spirit, teaching them to observe all that I have commanded you; and lo, I am with you always, to the close of the age (Matt. 28:18-20).

13
More Than Human
(Acts 1:6-11)

Christianity begins and ends with a Person. The core of Christianity is not a proposition but a Person. The heart of the Christian message is not an ideology but a Man, the God-Man. The ground of faith is neither ethics nor theology, but the Savior, who was human, yet more than human. Although Jesus was *more* than human, He was *at least* human and, presumably, worked through all those critical passages that precisely make me human. Because Jesus is more than human, we cannot psychoanalyze Him as if He were merely the most perfect human. But, just because He is human, we are allowed to wonder how He handled the challenge of living and dying as perfectly as possible. Thus, I felt the need for a concluding word on that truth.

Jesus was a Man unlike any other who ever lived before or followed after. He was completely unique. His character was unimpeachable. His teaching was the highest and finest human minds have ever contemplated. Born in a stable out of wedlock, raised in a carpenter's home in Nazareth (from which people believed nothing good could come), He was rejected in His life's work, His own special contribution to humanity. He tried to help a man on the sabbath and got attacked for it. He encouraged a paralytic, forgave his sins, and was opposed. He healed a blind man and barely escaped stoning. He offered love and received hate. He spoke the truth and heard it called lies; sowed mercy and
114

reaped judgment; brought salvation but got a cross. Even His own friends betrayed Him.

He was handed over to the government. The governor said, "I find in him no fault at all" (John 18:38, KJV). Yet he had Jesus beaten and scourged, and released a genuine criminal in His place. Again Pilate said, "I find no crime in him" (John 19:4). Then the governor washed his hands, had Jesus nailed to a cross, sealed Him in a tomb, and set up guards at the burial site.

Misunderstood, hated, despised, rejected—in three short years evil did its work. But it wasn't enough. It would have been for the rest of us. But Jesus, human though He was, was more than human. He burst the bonds of death and came forth from the tomb on the third day. His victory was so radical, unexpected, and complete that no friend or foe, priest or Pharisee, disciple or procurator, life or death, could keep Jesus down. Finally, He ascended; He just kept going up from the Mount of Olives. I can only tell you what happened. "And when he had said this, as they were looking on, he was lifted up, and a cloud took him out of their sight" (Acts 1:9). So Christianity began with *that kind* of Person.

The church in Indiana where I was pastor during seminary days was located in the country. Typically, it had a graveyard behind it. We used to walk around the tombstones searching for those with the oldest dates. I'll never forget one particular marker, because it didn't have the usual "Born" and "Died" written on it. Rather, it said: "Born - 1830"—"Ascended - 1902." The family of this person couldn't bring themselves to inscribe *Died* on the tombstone of their loved one. They chose the word *ascended* instead.

This is how some are able to think at death. But they wouldn't be so sure of their upward track if they did not believe their Lord went up before them.

The Ascension of Christ

That's why the ascension of Jesus is special to so many. Different minds will always be attracted to different parts of the story of Jesus. One comes under the spell of His birth. Another is gripped by the passion. But at least a few, myself among them, if they had a choice to build a tabernacle on their favorite spot, would not choose Bethlehem, Nazareth, Mount Tabor, or Calvary. They would choose Mount Olivet, because from there you can see the furthest. From the Mount of Olives you can look into the opened heavens above and round about on the waiting world with its multiple tasks, and then back upon a mysterious wonder of a finished redemption.

The ascension of Jesus took place from the Mount of Olives. Even though it is like a second resurrection, the ascension has never been standard procedure for many Christians. It is not mentioned that often in the New Testament. It falls on a Thursday in the church calendar. It takes place between Easter and Pentecost. It was the last of a series of appearances and disappearances of Jesus, which symbolized His return to the eternal realm from which He came (John 1:1).

An Up-and-Down Religion

There's a lot of motion and movement going on here. That makes ours an up-and-down religion. Christian theologians have given it a big name, like *incarnation* (or Christmas, to most folks). But God comes down to His children through His Son and becomes part of life in our world. So God is up and you and I are down. Then Christ comes down too. Then He goes back up where He came from.

Recall Jesus' words in John's Gospel: "I have *come down* from heaven, not to do my own will, but the will of him who sent me; . . . For this is the will of my Father, that every one who sees the

Son and believes in him should have eternal life; and I will *raise him up* at the last day" (John 6:38-39, author's italics).

Paul put it like this:

> Have this mind among yourselves, which is yours in Christ Jesus, who, though he was in the form of God, did not count equality with God a thing to be grasped, but *emptied himself,* taking the form of a servant, being born in the likeness of men. And being found in human form he *humbled himself* and became obedient unto death, even death on a cross. Therefore God has highly *exalted* him and bestowed on him the name which is above every name, that at the name of Jesus every knee should bow, in heaven and on earth and under the earth, and every tongue confess that Jesus Christ is Lord, to the glory of God the Father (Phil. 2:5-11, author's italics).

Emptied, humbled, then exalted. Ours is an up-and-down religion!

These are the terms we use to describe the activity of humanity and the divine, and I can't think of a better way to portray what is meant. In one sense it seems simplistic to say God is up there, or "thither," as the King James Bible renders it. (I love that word *thither.* Just to say it suggests ethereal flight. It's more than just "there.") *Thither!* God is everywhere and is not to be localized. To say God is up means He is far above us, beyond us, and is so much greater than we are, but not so far beyond us that He would have nothing to do with us. That's what the coming of Christ was about.

Because Jesus was willing to be the lowliest human—taking the form of a servant, He was also more than human. In truth, no one can say why Jesus is either human or divine or how much He is of each. We can only celebrate our faith that He is, and then go on to tell the story of what He did.

The ascension is part of that story. *Ascension* is a symbolic word describing a higher level of being than our earthly existence can provide. From that level of existence Christ came, to that level He belongs, and in that level He now reigns in exaltation.

There is something of cosmic proportions at work here; something too grand to be limited to our earthbound categories. Luke's word *ascension* is a poetic expression used to depict a divine event that cannot be fully grasped by men and women. We need not be too concerned whether the terms *up* and *down* are accurate. For I have discovered that it is not in heaven that we find God. It is in God that we find heaven.

Some things we can know about the ascension. Jesus ascended as a glorified human being: "This Jesus" (v. 11). "Jesus, . . . in the same way," that is, as a human being, but more than human. This same Jesus, glorified, but still the same Jesus—carpenter's Son, teacher, crucified, and suffering One. The same Jesus has now gone up and is seated at the right hand of the Creator. This same Jesus, the One who was rejected by the establishment, tried by Pilate, crucified by Rome, buried in a borrowed tomb, raised from the grave—to this suffering One God has said, "Sit at my right hand,/ till I make your enemies your footstool" (Ps. 110:1). This Jesus has ascended to be with God, and, "All power is given unto me" (Matt. 28:18, KJV), He said.

This Jesus was taken up, ascended—not to forsake us but to continue to redeem us. The One who came and stood beside us, who suffered because of us and for us, who felt the heavy hand of Caesar, the fickleness of the mob, the cowardice of His disciples —this One has gone up! He is more than human, not only for the church which worships Him, but for the whole world which must bow the knee.

A New Beginning

The ascension of Jesus marks the beginning of something brand new in religious history. "It is to your advantage that I go away" (John 16:7), He said. The absence of Christ means a new form of His presence, to be signaled by the coming of the Spirit. Jesus went away so He could be really present—in Birmingham, in South Africa, in Nicaragua, and in Moscow . . . so that He could be present on both sides of every curtain we erect.

Notice that "a cloud received him out of their sight" (Acts 1:9d, KJV). At the very moment we want Jesus to be most real, something obscures Him. All things come and go in life. People are doing either one or the other. Jesus came down to Bethlehem and went back up from Mount Olivet. For forty days He and His disciples had enjoyed fellowship together, knowing who He was and what His will was, and now, with an irony almost crueler than the crucifixion, Jesus was taken up and away from them. Just when it appears that Jesus takes off when you need Him most, and the faithful appear to be abandoned, sometimes there is an unrecognized blessing in the going.

I remember when my parents took me as a child to Boy Scout camp one summer and what I felt when they went home without me. "A cloud received" them out of my sight, and there I stood by myself. It was the first time I was away from home on my own and I was terrified by their absence. But now I see how their going was for my own good. It allowed me the opportunity to learn to live with my contemporaries, how to compete, how to carry my own share of the load, and how to get along relationally without the constant protective presence of my mom and dad.

At the ascension, Christ disappeared to put the disciples on their own. He did this because God wants persons, not puppets. Yet, there is a paradoxical sense in which, by going away, Jesus did not go away at all. He who once dwelt *among* them now dwelt *within* them through the Spirit of God. He was more available than before, which meant they had access to the presence of God wherever they were.

Here's a paradox: after the ascension, Jesus was never more present than when He was absent! That is true of all deep relationships in life. One day they will reach a state which transcends time and space. May that not be something that the Bible calls *heaven?*

But the ascension is not just an essay about the future. It is not bon voyage to Jesus. It is not an invitation to "fly the friendly skies!" It has a downward, earthly dimension as well, and that is where you and I come in. Just as those poor disciples collected their wits about them and set about the dreary task of living until the kingdom comes, they heard: "He is not here: for he is risen" (Matt. 28:6, KJV). That is not just resurrection-morning rhetoric. That is the description of human reality: what Paul meant when he said, "We know that the whole creation: has been groaning in travail together until now" (Rom. 8:22). And that word *groaning* is as earthbound and powerful in anticipation as *thither* is ethereal. How real it is! How do we cope with the "downside" of glory?

In the midst of their groaning they heard, "Men of Galilee, why do you stand looking into heaven?" That was not so much a question as it was a rebuke. Consternation, wonder, and awe are things that liberate the imagination. They remind us of the promises and make us intimate with the divine. They are not luxuries in the economy of salvation, but necessities. In and of themselves, they are not sufficient. Doubtless, the apostles would gladly have gone up into the clouds with the Lord. Given the choice to return to the mundane world of Galilee or partake of the glories of heaven, who wouldn't? Neither they nor we are permitted the luxury of gazing at Jesus' feet. "Why do you stand looking into heaven?" Get on with it! Stop looking up "thither" and start looking on earth for evidence of the rule of Christ.

"I will not leave you comfortless" (John 14:18, KJV), says Jesus. I will not leave you without assistance. On Pentecost we celebrate the coming of that assistance, namely, the present tense of God, a new kind of Emmanuel, God with us. Despite the tremendous odds and every indication to the contrary, we are not alone! God has given us several things with which to carry on His work.

He Has Given Us the Spirit

He is the presence of God, who is a reminder of what *was* and the sign of what *is to be* while He aids us in managing what *is.* The Spirit of God strengthens us and fortifies us to do what needs to be done.

He Has Given Us the Church

It is the body of His fellowship whose service to the Word and ministry transcends the boundaries of time and the frailties of the human condition. I am confessing my own faith here. I was raised in the church. I can never recall a time when the church was not part of my life. So I know it from within.

I am aware of the accusations and criticisms made against the church and some of them are true. But I declare to you in the words of William Cowper, who first spoke them about England, "O Church, with all thy faults, I love thee still."[1] You have to come to terms with imperfection to be able to say that. Once you realize that church is just people who have responded to Christ in varying degrees of intensity and none of them have arrived yet, the notion of a perfect institution or ideal religious community is bound to disappear.

I learned to be more tolerant of the local church once I realized it should consist of all kinds of people, and you don't choose your fellow church members as you do your friends. They are given to you. Thus, I have grown to love the diversity of the church. I am touched by the signs of grace we receive and by the lives that are changed, friendships formed, forgiveness experienced, and children nurtured into the faith. I marvel at the many ways in which people respond to the call to minister to others in Jesus' name. I am excited by the strength of the spiritual ties that hold together people of widely different temperaments and opinions. And I rejoice that in spite of all the failures, the Spirit does offer in a living church the supportive fellowship that we all need. I love the church because, with all her faults, Christ has chosen this instrument to be His body on earth to love those in need and open doors to receive all who respond to His gospel.

God has left us His Spirit, His church, and one another precisely because Christ has gone up. Because Christ has gone up, we can inscribe *ascended* on our tombstones. Because Christ has gone up, the church has something to say to life down in the valley. To those alienated in their family life, the church says Christ has ascended. To the person with terminal illness, the unemployed, the street people, the suffering, let Christians say to them what He said to us, "I am ascending to my Father" (John 20:17). To those first disciples who feared His leaving, Jesus assured them He was not going away but up. It ought to be a source of strength to those of you who find yourselves caught in the ordinary human dreariness of life, that the One who became so much like us has gone up to take charge with the One who made us. Christ has ascended!

I am struck by how the beautiful things of life are built right into the ugly. Both joy and flowers grow in the dirt. Such is life. Jesus experienced the dirt as well as the joy. It was in the wilderness of temptation where we found out the kind of character Jesus had. If goodness were simple and easy then we would never know what we were made of either. Temptation is the occasion to test our mettle, burn off the dross, purify our intentions, evaluate our motives, and to see what we really live for.

If you have never been seriously tempted, either you are singularly graced, or you have missed the whole point of living. But if you have known temptation, then you know that faith is doubt overcome.

Jesus learned in Gethsemane how flowers grow in the dirt of loneliness. Without loneliness, we would never come to know who we are. Loneliness is that feeling that we do not belong, while at the same time feeling as if we absolutely must belong. Loneliness forces us into isolation to discover who we are without others, so we can offer ourselves to others in good faith.

If you have never been desperately lonely, either you are singularly graced, or you have never met yourself. But if you have been lonely, then you know that belonging is isolation overcome.

Jesus saw life bloom in the dirt of failure in Nazareth because it was there that He ran into limitations. Failure shoves us back down to the earth from which we leap. Failure humiliates our human pride. It reminds us that we cannot do everything.

If you have never failed, either you are singularly graced, or you have never attempted anything of consequence. But if you are familiar with failure, then you realize that success is defeat overcome.

Joy grows in the dirt of suffering. Suffering is a peculiarly human experience. Animals can know pain, but humans know hurt. That knowledge transforms pain into suffering. Jesus recognized it as God's best disguised gift to human beings. Patiently endured, suffering engenders that rare human quality of gentleness. When we are flayed about by circumstances beyond our control or by sin or stupidity within our control, we get tenderized a bit.

If you have not suffered in your life, you are either singularly graced, or you have not engaged life fully. But if you have suffered deeply, then you know that gentleness is suffering overcome.

On the third day Jesus saw resurrection bloom out of the dirt of crucifixion. The cross is the sign of contradiction in our lives. It is that point of existence where our horizontal pursuit of pleasure runs into our vertical thrust toward greatness. The cross is always situated in the deepest part of all of us, where our personal demons and doves clash for mastery. In this deadly cross fire, life's ultimate tensions are resolved. There in our own personal Gethsemanes, God's will and our own will intersect.

If you have never been crucified, either you are singularly blessed, or you have not strongly struggled with anything that mattered. But if you have experienced your own cross, then you know that peace is the cross overcome.

Now all of us are tempted: we get lonely, we suffer and fail. We rise to a degree of faith, belonging, success, and tenderness. But imagine Jesus, who was human but more than human, who endured the rawness of life to the fullest, who was tempted of the devil, burdened with suffering, so lonely that not a single person understood Him, and thought to be a failure in the most important mission of His life.

In the prime of life, Jesus got run over by it, bludgeoned to death, and hung out to dry. Where is the joy in that? Only in resurrection as death overcome. In His death He was transformed to new life. In His ascension, He is finally and absolutely free to enliven everyone; free to roam the cosmos; free from the first century on the Mount of Olives all the way to eternity! Jesus bounced down off the bottom of hell and sprang up to the highest heaven. Now that is real joy! And that is the message of ascension.

Because we are His brothers and sisters, we can do that too. So don't put "Died" on my tombstone. I prefer "Ascended!" "When he had said this, as they were looking on, he was lifted up, and a cloud took him out of their sight" (Acts 1:9). Out of sight!

Notes

Introduction

1. Guenter Rutenborn, *The Sign of Jonah,* (New York: Thomas Nelson & Sons, 1960), pp. 80-82.

Chapter One

1. Phillips Brooks, "O Little Town of Bethlehem," *Baptist Hymnal,* (Nashville: Convention Press, 1975), p. 85.

Chapter Three

1. Scott Peck, *People of the Lie,* (New York: Simon and Schuster, 1983), p. 269.
2. Ibid., p. 269.

Chapter Four

1. Lofton Hudson, *Grace Is Not a Blue-Eyed Blond,* (Waco: Word Books, 1968), p. 22-23.

Chapter Five

1. Arthur F. Sueltz, *Deeper Into John's Gospel,* (New York: Harper & Row, Publishers, 1961), p. 150.
2. James E. Dittes, *When the People Say No,* (New York: Harper and Row, Publishers, 1961), p. viii.
3. Walter D. Wagoner, *Mortgages on Paradise,* (Nashville: Abingdon, 1981), p. 75.
4. Dittes, p. 8.
5. *The New Merriam-Webster Pocket Dictionary,* (New York: Pocket Books, 1964), p. 321.
6. Wagoner, p. 79.

Chapter Six

1. Antoine De Saint-Exupery, *The Little Prince,* (New York: Harcourt & Brace Jovanovich, Publishers, 1943), p. 67-68.

Chapter Seven

1. Andrew D. Lester, *Coping with your Anger,* (Philadelphia: Westminster, 1983), p. 15.
2. Pat McCloskey, *When You are Angry with God,* (New York: Paulist Press, 1986), p. 2.

Chapter Eight

1. Donald E. Wildmon, *Stand Up to Life,* (Nashville: Abingdon, 1975), p. 15-16.

Chapter Nine

1. "Oliver North Hero," *The Birmingham Post-Herald,* 12 July 1987, p. A5.
2. Eric Berne, *Games People Play,* (New York: Grove Press, Inc., 1964), p. 87.

Chapter Eleven

1. R. Benjamin Garrison, *Are You the Christ?,* (Nashville: Abingdon, 1978), p. 7.

Chapter Twelve

1. John Pennington, "Pastor's Reflections," *Church Chronicle,* 13 Apr. 1987, p. 2.

Chapter Thirteen

1. David H. C. Read, *Unfinished Easter,* (New York: Harper & Row Publishers, 1978), p. 18.